The Winds Call No Man Sir

FootSteps Press
Kernow

The Winds Call No Man Sir

FootSteps Press First Edition
www.footsteps.co

Typeset by Daniel Nanavati

Photographs
© Anna McDougall/Nostalgic Bude
© Dr Bob Willingham
© Jonathan Ball
© Joseph Bonnici & Michael Cassar
© The Adrian Abbott Collection
© Frost Family Archive
© The Cornish / Hemmerle Family Archive
© Truro School

Cover Photograph: of Barrel Rock from RIBA 'Spirit of Place' Exhibition
"All down the sounding shores of Bude and Bos," Tennyson - Idylls of the King
© Dr Bob Willingham

ISBN 978-1-908867-29-2

The Winds Call No Man Sir

Cornish Childhood Days

Jonathan Ball

Jonath Ball

Photographs

Chapters

'Most Beautiful Bude, the Gem of the West'
Southern Railway poster by Sir Alker Tripp from 1947, the year of my birth.
Original poster Ball family Archive

Foreword

'Bude! Bude? I don't think I have ever been to Bude'.

'I am utterly astonished to hear you say that, Your Grace', is my reply. 'Bude is the centre of the universe, the entire world revolves round Bude and the sun never stops shining there.'

It is 5th November 1987 and Robert Runcie, Archbishop of Canterbury, is paying a pastoral visit to Cornwall. In reply to the question, 'What do you want to do during your visit, Your Grace' came the reply, 'I would like to meet the Coxswains and Senior Helmsmen of all the Cornish Lifeboats'. And so it was. There we are, all lined up in a row on the quay at Falmouth, in a gale of wind, white shirts, blazers, Lifeboat ties and grey flannels. Up the line comes Robert Runcie Archbishop of Canterbury, dear Peter Mumford, Bishop of Truro, together with the Divisional Inspector of Lifeboats John Unwin, who stopping opposite me roars 'Ball! Bude! prompting his Grace's comments and my reply.

As a retired Lifeboatman my best advice is when you come to Bude, and visit our fine town you must, you should come by road. Believe me, the majestic Atlantic rollers and lee shore of North Cornwall present the most hazardous of approaches from the seaward. If, however, despite my advice, you choose a seaborne entry you round Barrel Rock, so named from the barrel navigation mark standing sentinel to guide and warn mariners, the most westerly of all interventions by mankind hereabouts and the spot I chose in 1974 to go down on one knee to propose to the lady who agreed to take my name.

Chapel Rock has its flagpole proudly bearing the Cornish flag of St Piran, the Patron Saint of Tinners, signalling notice to all visitors of the fact that you have arrived in a Celtic land of myths and legends and saints aplenty. It is said this was home to the Venerable Bede, after which Bede Haven got its name, transmogrifying to Bude Haven and further abbreviated with the loss of the word 'Haven' in the 18th Century or thereabouts – heaven knows why because haven it is.

The town's fabled attractions were never better trumpeted than in the souvenir brochure prepared by the Directors of the London and South Western Railway to celebrate the opening of the final section of track from Holsworthy to Bude in August 1898.With culture and climate hand in hand the document starts with a quotation from Alfred, Lord Tennyson's "Idylls of the King"

> But after tempest, when the long wave broke,
> All down the sounding shores of Bude and Bos
> There came a day as still as heaven, and then
> They found a naked child upon the sands
> Of wild Dundagel , by the Cornish sea:
> And that was Arthur, and they foster'd him
> 'Till he by miracle was approved King.

But it was climate and the health-giving properties that had made their investment a duty as much as a privilege, acknowledging that 'Breezy Bude as it is so widely known, having already made a name for itself in the past has a still grander future before it as a first-class watering place' . The brochure goes on to detail that 'Bude has a climate of more than ordinary note' and, without letting the truth get in the way of a good line adds, 'so long as simple sanitary precautions are observed in Bude and Stratton no disease can live there'.

Bude Lifeboat Station is close by a crescent of demountable beach huts, and half way along is Summerleaze Beach Hut Number 31 where much time has been spent dreaming my dreams overlooking the breakwater and Barrel Rock. This hut is 3 minutes 26 seconds stroll westwards from my office, The Belvedere, where, from 1974 to 2001, I was head of a latter day James Herriot style architectural practice taking on all projects, great and small. Architectural practice gave way to the Co-creation of the Eden Project.

I am first and foremost a Cornishman, of and for my community. Bude has been very kind to me and rich in opportunity. It has been home since my birth in 1947 and is where, unfailingly, I have always celebrated Christmas.

This memoir is an intimate reflection of my early years. The evanescence of memory has been the spur, my grandchildren the motivation.

Jonathan Ball
The Belvedere
January 2015

For
Piran
Lamorna, Alexander

Photograph Dr Bob Willingham

I

Wroes
18 The Strand

The Strand, Bude c1956. Wroes Ladies Outfitters with 18 The Strand, accommodation over, adjacent to Southern National Bus Garage and Cook's Stores.

18 The Strand Bude is a flat over the shop and is home for the Ball family since our relocation to Bude in 1946 the year before I am born, my brother Chris and sister Jenny having both been born in Plymouth. Well, actually, it's a maisonette with two floors of accommodation together with winding stairs up to an attic that after several years becomes my playroom. Our home is south facing overlooking the River Neet and near to the middle of the town. Our front door is up a high-sided, dark alleyway off the pavement and also serves as the back door to the shop linking commerce to accommodation. Steep brown lino-covered stairs arrive at the first floor with kitchen and larder north facing to the right and dining room and sitting room to the left. Beyond the kitchen there is a further flight of stairs leading to the three bedrooms and small bathroom with toilet that serves all the occupants.

Dad had answered an advertisement placed in the Western Morning News by the Blanchminster Charity of Bude on the same day as parting company with his former employer, Dingles of Plymouth, which was being rebuilt following the Plymouth blitz. Dad did not share the view of the bright new Dingles future set out by the Directors in the brave new City mapped and reshaped by Professor Patrick Abercombie.

Mum and Dad married quietly on 19th February 1935 without even a photographer present. These were times when married women were not allowed to work and, whilst Dad is 11 years older than Mum his wages at the time were modest. Mum's book keeping skills secured her a job under her maiden name at the United Hunts' Club in Grosvenor Street, London where she was employed full time administering the gambling chitties from club members and those with whom reciprocity existed. Although throughout her life she has refused to be drawn, it was here that she witnessed what she referred to as pre-abdication 'goings

Macartney, McElroy and Co. My grandfather John Francis Macartney went into business with Joseph Aloysius McElroy, an American engineer who had come to Britain in 1899. In 1903 the company was appointed to design, construct and operate the Malta tramway system. My grandfather, centre front in grey Homburg, with McElroy to his left with cane. Company's photograph taken on the occasion of McElroy's departure from Malta to conduct important company business overseas. May 25th 1903, ten years before my mother's birth.
Photo, The Malta Tramway and Barracca Lift, Joseph Bonnici & Michael Cassar.

on' between the Prince of Wales and Wallis Simpson which made an indelible mark upon her.

Mum was born in Sleima, Malta on 19 September 1913 to Ethel Mary Georgina Cooper and John Francis Macartney, an eminent engineer who after leading the electrification of the Glasgow trams was awarded the concession to build and operate the Malta trams and also the Barracca Lift in Valletta – an admired landmark; a vertical lift connecting the public gardens of the capital city to the notorious harbour side entertainment district carrying the long affection of all passing British servicemen. Ethel's parents, my great grandparents, were splendidly redolent of the

The Barracca Lift. On Christmas Eve 1903 my grandfather was granted the contract to build this electrically powered lift linking the Barracca Gardens to the notorious harbour side district of Grand Harbour so beloved of British Servicemen.
Photo, postcard, Ball family archive

high Victorian age their names being Harry Horatio Theodore Cooper and Maud Selina Plenty Cooper.

Alas, John Francis Macartney died of a stroke months before Mum was born, his funeral procession being of more than a mile in length and securing extensive coverage in The Times of Malta. His untimely demise resulted in a contested Will which ended in the Royal Courts of Justice in The Strand, London, a place I was to get to know well some 90 years later. The Judgment went against them leaving mother and daughter in reduced circumstances. In 1919 Mum sailed out of Valletta Harbour travelling with her adored grandfather for England and a new home in Devonport, Plymouth. A good education at Devonport High School and Skerries College Plymouth, all paid for by kindly Uncle Jack, saw Mum securing her first job with the Bowring Press in Plymouth and then to Bude in 1931 where she was employed as book keeper at the Bude Steam Laundry. And so began our family Bude history. Mum lodged in The Crescent with the grand mother of Peter Cloke. Peter, who was to play such a great part in the formation of Surf Lifesaving in Great Britain, was a Lifeguard hero of my childhood years.

In contrast my father's early years had not enjoyed such educational

AMERICA.

POWER STATION — BUFFALO S™ RY. C°: 5000 H.P. DESIGNED BY J.A.McELROY M.E. OVERHEAD LINES DESIGNED & BUILT BY J.F.MACARTNEY EE

POWER STATION — BRIDGEPORT CON. 3000 H.P. OVERHEAD AND TRACK CONSTRUCTION, DESIGNED AND ERECTED BY J.A.McELROY EE CHIEF ENGINEER.

NORFOLK VIRGINIA. POWER STATION 1500 H.P. TRACK AND OVERHEAD CONSTRUCTION 30 MILES ALSO 50 CARS INSTALLED AND OPERATED BY J.F. MACARTNEY AS CHIEF ENGINEER AND GENERAL MANAGER.

NEW BRUNSWICK TRAMWAYS AND ELECTRIC LIGHTING. SYSTEM — 26 MILES OF TRACK, CARS, CABLES, LIGHTING STATION. INSTALLED BY MACARTNEY McELROY & C° AS CONSULTING ENGINEERS.

HIGHLANDS AND NEW PALTZ. TRAMWAY SYSTEM DESIGNED. INSTALLED AND OPERATED BY MACARTNEY McELROY & C°. AS CONSULTING AND CONTRACTING ENGINEERS.

SYRACUSE AND SURBURBAN. ELECTRIC RAILWAY OPERATED BY WATER POWER, DAM BUILT AND DESIGNED COMPLETE SYSTEM INSTALLED BY MACARTNEY McELROY & C°

MIAMI VALLEY TRACTION C°ˢ LINES. BUILT AND INSTALLED BY MACARTNEY McELROY & C°.

HOOZICK FALLS AND BENNINGTON VERMONT ELECTRIC TRAMWAYS — BUILT AND DESIGNED BY MACARTNEY McELROY AND C°.

REFERENCES.

ABILITY.

A.WILKIE ESQ. CHAIRMAN TRAMWAYS COMMITTE ABERDEEN SCOTLAND

J.YOUNG ESQ GENERAL MANAGER GLASGOW CORPORATION TRAMWAYS. SCOTLAND.

J.H.COX ESQ. CITY ENGINEER. BRADFORD ENGLAND.

F.H. DUNSFORD ESQ. MAYOR & CHAIRMAN TRAMWAYS COMMITTE. SOUTHAMPTON. ENGLAND

H.KIMBER ESQ ALDERMAN AND CHAIRMAN OF TRAMWAYS COMMITTEE. PORTSMOUTH ENGLAND

H.BUCKWELL ESQ MAYOR BRIGHTON ENGLAND

W.B.ROMMEL ESQ GENERAL MANAGER AND CHIEF ENGINEER LISBON PORTUGAL.

J FLETCHER ESQ BOROUGH. ELECTRICAL ENGINEER DURBAN NATAL

K.F.CAMPBELL ESQ BOROUGH ENGINEER HUDDERSFIELD.

FINANCIAL.

BANK OF BRITISH NORTH AMERICA.

CAPITAL AND COUNTIES BANK L™. LONDON AND BRANCHES.

MANCHESTER AND COUNTY BANK L™.

HALIFAX COMMERCIAL BANKING C° L™.

LONDON AND COUNTY BANKING C° L™.

YORKSHIRE AND BANKING C° L™.

LONDON CITY AND MIDLAND BANKS L™.

BANK OF SCOTLAND.

THE

LISBON TR
OF OVERHEAD
MACARTNEY McEL

OPORTO — POR
DESIGNED FOR

BUENOS AYR
OVERHEAD MATE
DESIGNED &
MACARTNEY Mc

MACARTNE
CONSULTING
53 V
LO
SP
TRAMWAY A

THE
SHERBROOKE Q
RAILWAY INCLUDING OVE
WATER POWER STA
MACARTNEY McELROY
HAMILTON RADIA
HAMILTON ONT
OVERHEAD CONS
AND CARS INSTAL

DURBA
COMPLETE OVERH
NOW BEING DESIG
MACARTNEY McELRO
56 MILES OF OVERHEA

Macartney, McElroy and Co Limited. My grandfather's company was registered in London on 26 April 1898 as an electrical, consulting, engineering and contracting firm. By the turn of the century the company had offices in London Westminster, Glasgow, Manchester, New York and Natal. They undertook contracts for municipal corporations throughout the United Kingdom and overseas including Durban and Natal South Africa, Lisbon Portugal,

RT OR WHOLE BY MESSRS
LTING & CONTRACTING ENGINEERS.

NENT.

60 MILES
AILWAYS BUILT BY
TP.

ERHEAD MATERIAL
OF ROAD.

CLORANO ST RYS.

MNS, ETC.
BY
P LTP

ROY & CP LTP
ACTING ENGINEERS.
ST.
S. W.

G PLANTS.

ES.

ANADA. 13 MILES
ANENT WAY, CARS.
ED AND BUILT BY

C RY.

RMANENT WAY &
POWER STATION.
TNEY McELROY & CP

AL.

INC STOCK CONTRACTS
PPLIED BY
TP.

52 CARS.

GREAT BRITAIN.

ABERDEEN. SCOTLAND: CARS, OVERHEAD SYSTEM, DESIGNED, SUPPLIED, & ERECTED, CABLES LAID BY. MACARTNEY McELROY & CP LTP.

GLASGOW. SCOTLAND THE COMPLETE DESIGNING SUPPLYING AND ERECTION OF 100 MILES OF OVERHEAD CONSTRUCTION. WHICH IS ONE OF THE LARGEST & MOST EFFICIENT SYSTEMS IN THE WORLD. THIS WORK HAS BEEN COMPLETELY CARRIED OUT BY US, IN ADDITION TO A LARGE PART OF THE PERMANENT WAY

WEST HARTLEPOOL. COMPLETE SYSTEM OF TRAMWAYS DESIGNED AND ERECTED.

BRADFORD YORKS. OVERHEAD CONSTRUCTION DESIGNED & ERECTED BY US.

SOUTHPORT LANCS. OVERHEAD CONSTRUCTION DESIGNED ERECTED & SUPPLIED BY US.

MANCHESTER LANCS. 20 MILES OF OVERHEAD CONSTRUCTION DESIGNED & BUILT BY US.

STOCKPORT LANCS. PERMANENT WAY FOR TRAMWAYS.

HUDDERSFILD YORKS. OVERHEAD CONSTRUCTION DESIGNED SUPPLIED & ERECTED BY US.

HALIFAX YORKS MATERIAL DESIGNED & SUPPLIED TO THE VALUE OF £10000.

ILFORD ESSEX. TRAMWAYS FOR THE URBAN DISTRICT COUNCIL THE COMPLETE OVERHEAD & PERMANENT WAY CONTRACT INCLUDING ALL THE SUPPLY OF ALL MATERIAL ETC.

BRIGHTON SUSSEX. PERMANENT WAY CONTRACT FOR ELECTRIC TRAMWAYS

PORTSMOUTH HANTS. OVERHEAD EQUIPMENT COMPLETE INCLUDING SUPPLYING & ERECTION OF MATERIAL.

SOUTHAMPTON. HANTS. SYSTEM OF OVERHEAD CONSTRUCTION DESIGNED SUPPLIED AND ERECTED COMPLETE.

POOLE AND DISTRICT RAILWAY. OVERHEAD AND PERMANENT WAY. CONTRACTS INSTALLED COMPLETE BY US.

NEWCASTLE ON TYNE THE COMPLETE WIRING OF CAR SHEDS.

HURST YORKS. OVERHEAD CONSTRUCTION FOR TRAMWAYS COMPLETELY INSTALLED BY US.

ASHTON - UNDER - LYNE. COMPLETE SUPPLYING AND ERECTION OF OVERHEAD EQUIPMENT.

ROCHDALE LANCS. THE COMPLETE ERECTION & SUPPLY OF THE OVERHEAD EQUIPMENT OF TRAMWAYS.

ROTHERHAM YORKS. THE COMPLETE SUPPLYING AND ERECTION NOW BEING PROCEDED WITH OF BOTH OVERHEAD AND PERMANENT WAY CONTRACTS. OF 16 MILLS (DOUBLE TRACK) ELECTRIC TRAMWAYS.

ETC.

Mozambique as well as extensive power station works throughout America and Canada. On the recommendation of the Crown Agents in 1903 the company was appointed to design, construct and operate the Malta tramways and Barracca Lift. Their contract, astonishingly, gave them a monopoly of electricity as the motive power in Malta.
    Photo, The Malta Tramway and Barracca Lift, Joseph Bonnici & Michael Cassar.

My grandparents Emma and Charles Henry Ball late 19th century Studio portrait taken by Hayman & Sons Launceston.

Photo Ball family archive

benefaction. Born in Launceston on 6th August 1902 into a large Cornish family several of whom had joined the Cornish Diaspora to far flung Dominions in hope and expectation of better opportunities than the modest prospects that prevailed in Cornwall. Father's formal education at the National School, an archetypal school house building still to this day bearing its stone carved title perched precipitously close by Launceston Castle, ended at the age of 14.

His father, my Grandfather Charles Henry Ball was himself born in Launceston on 1 December 1857, 12 days after the relief of the siege of the British Residency at Lucknow defended by the Duke of Cornwall's Light Infantry and which brought to an end the Indian Mutiny.

My grandmother, Emma Blatchford was born on 16 April 1860 at Tregeare near Egloskerry, a village four miles to the west of Launceston where my great-grandfather, Samuel Blatchford was bailiff to Squire Lethbridge on the Tregeare Estate. She was 23 when her first born, Frederick Blatchford Ball arrived in1883 and 42 years of age when my father, her 11th child arrived in 1902. All her children were born before the first manned flight by the Wright Brothers and even her youngest,

Dad, was of an age to witness the first motor car arriving in Launceston

Dad, being the youngest of the family, displayed a lifetime's reluctance to stray far from his Cornish roots, but by necessity London was to be home for his early working life. By the mid 1930s Dad had left London for Dingles of Plymouth where his sister Winifred was a fashion buyer in the ladies section and had secured a job with prospects for her baby brother, only just the wrong side of the River Tamar.

And so a combination of the Plymouth Blitz and an advertisement in the Western Morning News led to an interview with the Senior Stockwarden of the Blanchminster Charity in Bude. Senior Stockwarden - what a wonderful and befitting name for the Chairman of Trustees of so ancient and glorious an institution. This Charity is thought to be the oldest charitable trust in Britain if not the world, originating in around 1421.

During the reign of Elizabeth 1 this Charity was the responsibility of the Eight Men of Stratton, "Stratton was a market town when Bude was but a fuzzy down." They were represented by two Stockwardens known as General Receivers. In Good Queen Bess's time the stock of Stratton Parish was bestowed for three purposes: 'About Her Majesty's service for the buying of armour and equipment of soldiers', 'For the Relief and Maintenance of the poor of the Parish' and 'For all things necessary for the Defence of the Parish.'

Mum and Dad found themselves across the large mahogany desk from the Senior Stockwarden. By happy chance this was none other than the kindly proprietor of the Bude Steam Laundry who had been Mum's employer in 1931. Over the centuries the charitable objectives had narrowed down to education and providing parochial assistance to local persons in Stratton and Bude parishes. Extensive commercial property holdings in the centre of Bude provides most of the charitable income.

The front of 18 The Strand Bude is unmistakeably of more recent origin. In the 1930s one of the largest fires in the town for many years resulted in partial demolition and rebuilding for the then tenant, a Mr George Wroe. With our new tenancy we inherit a legend.

The mid 1930s saw Mr Wroe on hard times. His emporium sold gramophone records, antiques and various nick knacks. His pride and joy were two magnificent leather wing armchairs for which Mr Wroe regularly refused offers to purchase. The shop had two window display areas fronting the pavement, with a central shop doorway set some 6ft in from the pavement. Above this entrance way was the name Wroes. Despite Mr Wroes departure this name was retained, my parents coming to an early conclusion that the trading name Wroes sounded far better than Ball's.

The eye catching chairs, to the astonishment of the local population, one day disappeared with the memorable conflagration following soon after. The landlords to the property, The Blanchminster Charity rebuilt the accommodation complete with new shop front and central doorway and trading soon resumed complete with the two magnificent wing armchairs reinstated.

At second floor level the two south facing bedrooms each have double French doors onto the new lead flat roof above the first floor sitting room which terminates in a parapet wall. This enclosed suntrap is the centre of our al fresco lives. My earliest photographs are of me sat on the potty here, and another of my old fashioned pram placed there each day for my afternoon sleep with me well strapped in so if I wake and sit up I can just peer over the masonry parapet for probably the best bird's eye view of the goings on in the town. All is well - me out in the fresh air safely above with Mum below attending to the customers.

During the summer months we are but a few yards from one of the two main comings and goings as the bus stop is at the end of The Strand, just a few yards from the shop front door. The Strand is the main thoroughfare to the town running adjacent to the River Neet and leads to Belle Vue which is the central business district.

The bus stop delivers happy, smiling holiday faces. The Royal Blue service arriving at The Strand is one of the moments of our day. Great pride is taken in these buses being immaculate in every way. Some of the Royal Blue buses have a sharks' fin profile at the rear accentuated by gleaming chrome, others have a vertical ladder up the rear to a shining roof rack upon which the visitors' brown leather suitcases arrive having travelled in the open air.

Across the dark alleyway from our back door our immediate neighbour is the bus depot and garage for Southern National with the manager's accommodation above. Beyond that is the renowned Cook's stores run by Ernie Yeo and his wife. This grocery store has much more to do with the Old Testament than the New yet once again, with shop front similar to Wroes, a central doorway leads to a black and white tiled floor. All the shop walls are lined with mahogany shelving with turned spindles and etched mirrors inset between the shelves. There are polished worktops with built in tea caddies displaying produce from all quarters of the British Empire. Mr Yeo is firmly in charge and everything is truly immaculate. Every customer is greeted cheerily and with full deference. The time of day is passed in a way that is unique to each of his valued customers.

The rules of Cook's Stores are rigorously applied by its proprietor. The banter is a legend in the town. Ernie Yeo always refers to his wife as Mrs Yeo and her reply is always 'Yes Mr Yeo'. Only Mr Yeo is allowed to use the bacon slicer, a magnificent piece of contemporary technology in rich maroon enamel and dramatic stainless steel circular cutting edge.

'Three slices of smoked ham please Mr Yeo'

'Certainly Mrs Yeo as soon as I have attended to Mrs Ball' and so it goes on.

Other protocols are strictly maintained. If you need lavatory paper Mrs Yeo is despatched to the store room at the back and emerges with the request covered in newspaper. A roll of toilet paper is never, never visible to the eye within the portals of this shop.

The most important of the customers are able to park their

Potty training on the flat roof. 18 The Strand 1948 Ball family Archive.

Strapped in for my afternoon's fresh air on the flat roof. In the distance Bencoolen Bridge 1948 soon to be demolished in favour of creating wider arches to accommodate the River Neet in spate. The bridge was deemed culprit for the regular flooding of all the houses in The Crescent, adjacent to the bridge, linking through to Bude Canal.

Photo Ball family archive

11

Ball family portrait, Dempster's photographic studio Bude, 1950.

Photo Ball family archive

The Strand c1950. From the east with tamarisk hedge and hawser from the wreck of the Bencoolen prior to Strand flood defence wall.

Photo the Adrian Abbott collection

cars immediately outside the shop on the Strand. Amongst Mr Yeo's most valued customers is Mrs Thynne the elderly surviving matriarch of a family that had once owned substantial holdings in the town. She lives at Penstowe Manor, Kilkhampton and in latter years a visit to Cook's Stores is one of her few outings each week. Her conveyance is an enormous limousine which is complete with chauffeur in peaked cap who is time serving and gives the impression of feeling badly treated by his employer.

He has an amusing way of getting his own back which delivers a weekly smile to those local residents in the know. The limousine has to be washed and polished for each outing. The chauffeur diligently polishes the side of the limousine from which Mrs Thynne enters and alights, with the chauffeur holding the door open and helping her over the running board. On the other side the mud splattering of months are plain for all to see except by the elderly matriarch. Mr Yeo, of course never lets on despite the deference in which Mrs Thynne is held.

At the east end of the Strand heading out of the town the road merges into Bencoolen Road which is named after Bude's most famous shipwreck. This end of the Strand holds a special affection. It is home to the Octagon Ice Cream Parlour which sells Eldorado ice creams, milk shakes and Knickerbocker Glories in tall fluted glasses. It is half way between home and the railway station and it is Heaven.

The most important accommodation at this end of The Strand, so far as we are concerned, is Behenna's Garage. This is where Dad keeps his pride and joy. We might be one of the last families in the business community of the town to be blessed with a television but we are right up there with the best of them when it comes to a motor car. Dad's pride and joy is black with dark green leather upholstery and is called a Ford Popular - registration LCV 673. It has shiny chrome bumpers and chrome front radiator grill and bright orange indicators that, when Dad throws a switch, pop out from the door frame and behind the ears of the front seat driver and passenger. The Ford Pop is primarily for our Sunday family outings, the only day of the week when Wroes is closed all day.

At Easter, in the summer and on Boxing Day these are often as not to Trevone Bay, near Padstow, to visit Aunty Wendy, Mum's sister, and Uncle Dick together with our cousins Geraldine and Richard. Trevone holds a special place in all our hearts, but most particularly in Mum's. With the Plymouth family home at Crownhill blitzed by the Luftwaffe it was to Trevone, close by Padstow, where Mum, Jenny and Chris were evacuated to a safe seaside haven far away from the bombs and Plymouth's perils.

We all love going to number 2 Atlantic Terrace, Trevone, a fine slated terraced building. During the war, Mum would cycle each week to pay the rent to the four Miss Marleys who lived in Edwardian splendour in nearby Melingy. They were the daughters of the Padstow Physican Dr Marley, friend of Charles Dickens and immortalized by him as Marley's ghost.

The Moorings had been purchased soon after the war by Wendy and Dick, or should I say Lieutenant Commander Hull RN as he is appropriately referred to by all. The Moorings is exactly that for the Hulls, with each naval leave finding them heading for Cornwall. Summer visits from Bude ensure any alcoholic shortcomings in our home experience are redressed. Dick is never happier than with a glass in hand and his solemn mission is to get one into Dad's within minutes of our arrival

Outings of any distance at other times of the year invariably involve visiting members of the Ball family, usually Aunt Edith. Edith Annie

2 Atlantic Terrace, Trevone, The Moorings front lawn, c1955. The Ball family have just arrived on a Sunday outing from Bude. Dad on left already with beer glass in hand courtesy of Uncle Dick, far right.

Photo Ball family archive

Ball lives an hour away in Truro and adores Dad, her baby brother and our move to Bude only came about through her and Aunty Win's financial support. She is large, twinkly eyed and jovial and a great story teller of the most gentle yarns. Our every arrival at Carnon Downs is greeted with ' Sadie! Bude's here....get the kettle on'.

Edie is so generous and big hearted. When Sadie Kempthorne's fiancé joined the Cornish Diaspora Edie asked her to move in as housekeeper. The fiancé had left to seek his fortune in the gold mines of South Africa, one of so many of his generation, giving rise to the adage that wherever in the world you find a large hole in the ground you will always find a Cornishman at the bottom of it!. He somehow forgot to return and make Sadie his bride. His loss, and hers, is our gain. Sadie makes Cornish seedy cake to die for.

Edie's husband is Billy Edwards, a kindly, gentle, Kipling-esque character who is content to spend time in his garden and have Edie's fulsome frame and personality fill the house. He works for the West Briton newspaper, a journal of great authority in the far west. This keeps Edie in a fund of stories and her best one is about a neighbour who

15

simply refused to accept the news that King GeorgeV1 had died until she had read it in The West Briton.

Our longest, but rare outings are to distant Fareham to visit Dad's other favourite sister Winifred. My sister Jenny is Aunty Win's favourite and whilst Aunty Edie will keep the weather eye out for Chris and me during our boarding school days at Truro, Jenny's secondary education is to be at Talbot Heath School for Girls in Bournemouth with Aunty Win close by to indulge her and be at hand if needed. Aunty Win always travels first class and given that this fact invariably attaches to each and every description of her when she comes into conversation, it says so much about us, the Bude branch of my far flung Ball family.

There is a particular characteristic to our Sunday outings. Mum has packed up the picnic but it is Dad who has the final say as to where we hold the picnic. He has three or four spots. They all involve bringing the Ford Pop to a halt right in the middle of a waterjump where a stream runs across the road, a common feature throughout the highways and byways of rural north Cornwall.

His two favourites are Crackington Haven where the road fords immediately at the back of the pebbled beach and was the destination of Mum's Southern National bus journey on the eve of my birth. Perhaps most favourite is the ford at Cansford on the A39 trunk road south of Bude on our way to Trevone. Here this waterjump that gives the locality its name sits in a gentle dip in the landscape with high hedges and hazel bushes and a rickety timber foot bridge that allows pedestrians to cross without getting their feet wet. We alight to picnic in rural idyll. We sit down to our bank side feast, Dad, with infinite care, washes the Ford Pop, totally oblivious to the occasional passing Sunday traffic splashing past on what is the main trunk road serving the coastal communities of north Cornwall.

The yellow and chrome Automobile Association members' badge mounted on the radiator gets a special polish. This ensures we receive a salute from the AA patrolling officers on their motor bikes with bright yellow side cars in serge tunics, with goggles and brown leather gauntlet gloves.

Just a little further on from Cansford waterjump, as Dad calls it, is Otterham Station and then the high ground of Davidstow. When Trevone bound we always accelerate along the high straight close by the disused World War Two airfield where in 1954 Bude hosts a Formula One motor racing event. But Dad's acceleration here has nothing to do with racing. We are just about to enter what, in his own words, is 'Dad's bit of velvet'. At the end of the high straight Dad turns off the engine and puts the Ford Pop into neutral and does not turn the engine on again until we cross Camelford Bridge. We have coasted the last couple of miles downhill and, in Dad's estimation, have saved at least two cupfuls of petrol.

Just occasionally, Dad will take a notion that a Sunday outing will not involve going to see relatives. It is August 1952 and something has happened, as unexpected as it is unwelcomed. It has become the lead story on our evening news on the wireless. It has happened on the north coast of Devon and is no farther than a Sunday's afternoon drive up the coast, over the border into Devon and beyond Clovelly where the paddle steamer takes us for outings to Lundy Island.

We are ever mindful of possible flooding and my school chum Paddy Frost and his family get flooded out regularly. The wireless is telling us that there has been a flood disaster at a place called Lynmouth, a coastal holiday resort, just like ours, but nestling below where high Exmoor meets the Atlantic Ocean. On brother Chris's persuasion Dad announces we will be driving up there to bear our own witness to this moment in history. This is a real adventure for us. Apart from anything else outings involve going down into Cornwall, not across into Devon.

My chum Paddy Frost 1951 on the end of Nanny Moores Bridge immediately outside his front door, looking across the River Neet to the tamarisk hedge and the Strand.

Photo Frost Family Archive

The Strand adjacent to Bude bus stop. The 1953 floods looking east to Behenna's Garage. The Bude bus carrying advertisement for Dinnis Medland & Co, Belle Vue, acquired by the Ball family in 1955.

Photo, the Adrian Abbott collection.

At our destination we gaze upon destruction such as I have never seen before. From high Exmoor we have descended towards the stricken town but only as far as a large bend in the road on our descent where there is a police road block. Even the police are different. The Devon Constabulary has a different policeman's helmet with a big chrome bobble on the top. Several policemen are there with walkie-talkie short wave wirelesses strapped to their backs. We do not linger long but if I close my eyes I can picture the bulldozers, the tree roots, the upturned battered cars, the destroyed buildings and the desolation.

II

Marina
102 Kings Hill Bude

Marina 102 Kings Hill, Bude before front hedge was removed and realigned for road improvements.

Photo Cornish/Hemmerle family archive

102 Kings Hill Bude, home to the Cornish family is a sturdy 1930s bungalow with asbestos slate hipped roof and Cornish dob render. It is on a bend of Kings Hill beyond where the pavement footpath runs out and marks the eastern extension of what the 1930s described as 'ribbon development'. It has a small front lawn and well kept hedge directly onto the tarmac road. It has a gravel driveway on the west boundary and is next to the boundary hedge that is so much thicker than the others. This was because it held a secret. The secret was that it had been significantly altered by the hand of man to accommodate the circumstances of the times just past. Its inconspicuous secret, modest in proportion, sturdy in construction reinforced with old lead waste pipes requisitioned for the purpose, and in modest subterranean splendour, was an air raid shelter. Down two or three steps, dark, smelly and scary with a single timber seat at its south end furthest from the doorway entrance. A never to be forgotten hidey hole, the purpose of its final years so much more frivolous than the reason which demanded its construction.

On the northeast corner of the front lawn built into the hedge is a delightful garden seat. This whole construction comprises four substantial flags of Trevillet rustic slate, buttressed by the encompassing hedge with enormous rounds of thrift, which we call sea pinks, to complete the picture and integrate the seat within the front hedge.

Climbing onto this seat at around five o'clock in the evening I stand, gazing westward down Kings Hill, looking and listening for the arrival home from work of George Alfred Cornish. George, a builder's labourer, air raid shelter constructor and front garden landscaper of Marina, patriotically named after Princess Marina, Duchess of Kent whose marriage coincided with the building of the bungalow. The putt putt of his small motor cycle overtures his arrival, unmistakeable weather

With Corky in the front garden of Marina, 1950.

Photo the Cornish/Hemmerle family archive

worn face, cap and Players cigarette in the corner of his mouth and his World War Two khaki haversack slung over his back with what remains of his 'croust'. Home from a day's labour and starving 'ungry.. I c.. c.. c.. could eat an 'oss and ch ch ch chase the rider'. George's wife Lillian becomes my second mother and in so doing secures a second name, Corky. Lillian is far too difficult for me to pronounce and I abbreviate Cornish to Corky.

Her new name soon secures wide currency in the town. Corky is matriarch of Marina in every sense. She is custodian of the budget, and woe betide George if his brown wage packet, small in size and modest in content, with name and calculations on the front is delivered to her opened.

Behind Marina the more extensive back garden, including a small triangular cut from the nearest adjacent field belonging to Farmer Vickery, is laid out to all the best arrangements for agrarian living and home grown produce sufficient to feed her family and the summer bed and breakfast visitors. The family move out of the bungalow for the main summer season, living in outhouses at the back. These are alongside the pig and the chickens which supplement the unopened wage packet to complete the modest budget upon which the Cornish family survives.

If it is meat on the table it is either chicken, rabbits shot with the 2.2 rifle or pork aplenty when the pig departs as the largest of the residents hereabouts.

Beyond one or two of Farmer Vickery's fields at the rear, runs the single track of the London and South Western Railway branch line to Bude, terminus with London Waterloo. Bude Railway Station is about a mile as the crow flies from Marina and adjacent to the bottom of Kings Hill and the Halt sign that marks its junction with the main road from Bude to Stratton.

We have a very special visit to the Railway Station once a year as an integral element of Marina's annual budge. It is always dark, the steam train puffs its way into the station substantially illuminated at eye level by hand held mobile oil lamps giving that special warm glow and distinctive smell. We gather at the iron gate, at the east end, looking towards the engine shed and turntable for the locomotives beyond the cattle and sheep pens which receive animals driven down from Stratton market. This is where the goods van is unloaded, not at the front entrance double doors through which the passengers depart. It is also next to the

Bude Station from the east at the Halt sign junction, bottom of Kings Hill.

Photo Adrian Abbott collection

siding for loading the upline Perisher.

The porter carefully handles the package for Cornish, Kings Hill. It is a large, flattish cardboard box, peppered with holes. Its contents, cheeping and chirping are a multitude of three day old chicks. The tiny chicks arrive as our new residents for 'growing away' and fattening for the summer B&B visitors. There is a special outhouse at Marina for their early days - a vast lamp held at low level on a wire which delivers sufficient heat and light to ensure their survival. A galvanised circular water container with Chinaman's hat keeps them watered, another for grain keeps them fed. The daily refilling of these is a job that falls to me.

They all end their days in the same manner. Close by the back hedge with the hawthorn and hazel is the remaining stump of an old washing line, a former telegraph pole. It has been sawn off about a foot above the pathway by George as it is unsafe. It is peppered with holes from endless target practice. Occasionally in the summer I help Corky to catch one of the chickens and together we control the flapping wings down to this telegraph stump. A swift, single blow wielded by Corky with the small firewood axe despatches life to feed the guests to make the ends meet.

Marina's front door becomes redundant with the end of the visitor season. The Bed and Breakfast sign on the front hedge with cup hooks suspending a second sign below confirming room availability, is packed away for another year as the autumn winds start to blow.

Adjacent to the porch is the first outbuilding built on the western boundary. It is a wash house where Corky keeps the mangle with its big revolving timber rollers along with the large galvanised tin bath with handles at each rounded end and hung up on the outside wall. It is used at weekends in front of the fire and filled with kettles of hot water. George keeps his cap on even when having his bath.

Corky and George have three children Jean, the eldest, then Micky and then Mary. Jean works in Duchy Bakeries shop on Belle Vue; Micky, carpenter and joiner, works alongside George for Parkhouse Bros from their workshops and builders' yard adjacent to the higher wharf of Bude canal. Mary works for Mum and Dad at Wroes in 18 The Strand.

Mary is the reason why Corky has become my second Mum. My own Mum does not enjoy the luxury of time to devote to a small child. She works all the hours she can to get the Ball family new business prospering despite the immediate post war privations and the restrictions of rationing which extend to clothing. The clothing coupons issued for us siblings are diverted to the good cause of securing profit for the shop. Mary suggests that her Mum might take Jonny out during the day in his pram, returning him when the shop shuts. This plan is soon successfully implemented.

But then there is a problem. It starts as a small problem but with the passing of weeks and months it gets bigger. Jonny does not want to come back to 18 The Strand when the shop shuts. He is happy playing in the front and back garden at Marina and on the beach at weekends and in the summer, the playground for the local population. I start staying overnight at Marina and soon I have two homes, two Mums and two families all treating me as their own.

Mickey's passion is motor bikes and after my Kings Hill sojourns, I sit on top of the petrol tank of

With Micky Cornish on his Royal Enfield motorbike. Marina, winter 1948-49.
Photo Cornish/Hemmerle family archive

German POWs inside Holsworthy Prisoner of War camp. Teddy Hemmerle top left. Handwritten names on reverse of photo.

Photo Cornish/Hemmerle family archive

his ex Army Royal Enfield motor bike, I lean forward and hold on for dear life with both hands, and am cradled in Micky's lap as he drives me back to 18 The Strand.

Jean has, for some time, been a talking point in the town. With her girlfriends, all giggly and fair, she would spend her weekend free time during the war years on Summerleaze Beach, Bude, a Cornish family tradition that was to endure throughout my own growing up years.

Ten miles inland from Bude, just beyond Tamarstone Bridge and into Devon, is Holsworthy, a market town and the centre for all livestock dealings throughout rural north Cornwall and north Devon. It had enjoyed strong commercial times through the First World War courtesy of the huge demand for home killed meat when German U boats were scoring great success in disrupting food supplies into Britain. Holsworthy has busy wars. The Second World War had brought another chapter in Holsworthy's history.

It was the local internment camp for aliens and Prisoners of War. Internment camps came in three grades, white, grey and black, white being the lowest security grade with the most relaxed arrangements, through to black which signalled a high security, boot camp regime. Holsworthy was a white camp. In Holsworthy was a young Luftwaffe navigator detainee, Helmut Hemmerle enjoying a low risk rating and despatched with others each Sunday to Summerleaze Beach Bude for a weekly swim and wash down in Bude Sea Pool.

An attachment began between Jean Cornish and Helmut Hemmerle, a mutual attraction that grew and was noticed, and with the notice came the wagging of tongues, and with the wagging of tongues comes trouble. Known to everyone as Teddy the quiet serving out of his prisoner of war time in Holsworthy was now in peril. Teddy, ever resourceful, personable and astute was well liked on both sides of the barbed wire encircling the prisoner of war camp. Amongst his friends was a fellow POW who had been elevated to trusted duties working in the camp office and was also driver to the camp Commander. Teddy was to get the nod that he was being moved out. The night before his scheduled departure he absconded - he went AWOL, absent without leave. He was a missing prisoner of war on the run, living off the land, hiding in hedges and ditches and foraging to sustain himself. After three days he eventually made his way under cover of darkness to Marina only to be caught by the Cornwall Constabulary who had staked out the bungalow.

A Court Martial the following day saw him before the Camp Commander, the splendidly named Colonel Bogey who lived in Killerton Road Bude. Teddy's friend, the Colonel's driver, enjoyed good terms with the camp Commander with Colonel Bogey establishing the Court Martial arrangements with scrupulous attention to propriety and fair play.

A German speaking Counsel was found and Teddy's pleadings heard.

Leading question from Colonel Bogey invited Teddy to confirm that it had been his every intention to return to the camp after seeing Jean. Teddy demurred - No, he said, ignoring the olive branch in the leading question, which was repeated as a mitigation offering that would allow a lenient determination. Teddy stood his ground, so did Colonel Bogey. The Court Martial found him guilty of absconding and he was given 28 days bread and water to be served out at a POW camp in Shaftesbury.

During the late war years Teddy and other POWs are deployed to spend working days on the land. A detachment is working on a farm near Gooseham in Morwenstow Parish. The mean minded farmer refuses their request of some milk from the farm for their tea and a tit for tat regime is established. Surreptitiously the POWs collect up as many eggs as they can find from the chickens.

At the end of the day's toil they quietly pass the eggs from their pockets to the British Army Sergeant in charge. Back on the trucks they are searched before returning to the camp. On arrival in Holsworthy half the eggs are retained by the guards and half returned to the prisoners.

With the Armistice came rules and regulations for any former prisoners of war wishing to remain in Britain. In essence, to stay in Bude Teddy had to endure two years hard labour on the land which he served out on a farm in Marhamchurch. These were hard times indeed. Long winters found Teddy in his Wellington boots stuffed full of straw in attempts to keep his feet warm.

Along with this he had to secure two stalwart citizens of Bude who would sign papers of surety and be responsible to the authorities for Teddy's conduct and behaviour. These were the local dentist Derek Ridler, who had won the Military Cross during the war, and the second citizen was a shop keeper from 18 The Strand, Bude, my Dad. In recognition of the privations Teddy is going through Dad donates his winter overcoat to him.

And so the necessities of time entwined the Ball family with the Cornish family in many ways. Dad secures Teddy a job with Ernie Woolacott who runs a local electrical business. When not being pushed in my pram by Corky I am often pushed by Jean and Teddy, married in 1948, and this time I am the reason for the tongues wagging again. 'Ahhh - I knew all along, Jean Cornish had to marry that Jerry'

But do spare a thought for Jean's Dad, George Alfred Cornish. George, whose entire life experience in geographical terms had been confined to west of the River Tamar, when war broke out found himself at Catterick learning to be a tank driver and soon to be deployed overseas to foreign fields for the first and the only time in his life. Unknowing at the time, George would find himself in a leading tank division on the D Day landings and through the liberation of Europe. Preparations at Catterick alarmingly involved the complete waterproofing of his Sherman tank suggesting to the tank crew that coming ashore in France would be perilous in every way. The Omaha landings were exactly that and on George's telling the beach became a graveyard for those tank crews that had been half hearted in their waterproofing preparations.

Cemented amongst the stories of my youth about the time I first knew the meaning of the word 'prostitute' is George's telling of a deployment to a French chateau one evening commandeered for the officers of his division. His sentry duty? To shepherd in the ladies of the night through the magnificent front door of the chateau which was then locked and barred with George spending the night with his Sherman tank reversed up to the front door. The gun barrel of the tank pointed menacingly down the front drive.

Even greater moments were to follow. George was in the first tank

Jean Cornish and Teddy Hemmerle on their wedding day 1948. Registry Office wedding Sturminster Newton, Dorset. Teddy in POW outfit on release from Motcombe Park POW camp Shaftesbury where he was serving out his Court Martial for absconding from Holsworthy POW camp to be with Jean.

Photo Cornish/Hemmerle family archive

corps to reach the Rhine. The retreating German forces had blown up the bridges and the Royal Engineers were called in to build a temporary pontoon bridge to get the tanks across the river. George was third tank in line. The pontoon bridge was assembled, the first Sherman tank despatched only to reach mid river when the pontoons parted and the tank pitched over, lost in the fast flowing waters of the Rhine with all crew.

The pontoons re-tethered by the Royal Engineers - tank number two moves cautiously forward only to suffer a similar fate. Again the engineers reconstruct the pontoon bridge and it is George Alfred Cornish on his first ever trip abroad who drives the first tank to cross the Rhine in the liberation of Europe.

It is four long years since leaving Cornwall that dear, stuttering, modest, unworldly George comes home to Marina only to find his eldest daughter Jean wants to marry ' a..f.. f.. f..**** German' when he has just spent the last four years of his life 'f.. f.. f.. fighting the buggers.'

George was honoured with the Belgian Croix de Guerre, with Palm, conferred by HRH Prince Regent of Belgium for ' courage and bravery in the glorious battles which led to the liberation of Belgium.' The insignia duly arrived by post at Marina, was opened and immediately put to flight, tossed across the kitchen floor...' better if they'd sent me a packet of fags...'

George 'Powder' Cornish. Sitting in Annie, Registration OW 8256 in Marina front drive.
Photo Cornish/Hemmerle family archive

An honour richly deserved and well intentioned I am sure, but they do not know Gunner 1089039 George Cornish as we do and as do his Bude workmates, who so enjoy his company for their days of labour together. How could they know that George is a man so well loved because of the complete absence of pomp and ceremony, of ego or malice, a man of so modest means but such wealth of contentment with his lot. In the shortest time George and Teddy become close life long friends. Just occasionally there is a self deprecating comment ...'I might be a rough old bugger, but I do like to drink from a nice glass'

Both Corky and George are as Cornish as the day is long. Corky is from the Sargent family of Marhamchurch and George from Falcon Terrace, Bude just along from the Falcon Hotel. George's father, Charlie, has also been a legend in the town. Charlie's first job after school was as billiard marker to serve the gentry staying at the Falcon Hotel. He is a great billiard and snooker man himself but it is for football that he is well known. From his own early years George is allowed in with his Dad to watch the billiards and to chalk the cues. It is from this that he secures his nickname 'Powder'.

Charlie maintains his athleticism well into late middle age when he is renowned as still being able to beat men half his age in a sprint. Having lost his first wife, George's Mum, he marries again in middle age. His bride, one of two spinster sisters living in the town, has never known a man. A Cornish family story that only comes to me in later years is of Charlie's telling. His second wife went to her grave without ever having experienced an orgasm. A virgin when she married in middle age, each time Charlie made love to her, she fainted.

Mary, George's younger daughter is also going to be married to Bertram Glibert a Belgian whose father has been none other than Foreign Secretary in the Belgian Government at the outbreak of war. He then moved his family to the Belgian Congo to keep them out of conflict's way.

Bertram's father did not survive the war and his mother soon remarries to a retired British Squadron Leader living in Breakwater Road Bude. Bertram is a photographer and soon finds work in the town with the local photography studio run by Frank Dempster. The early post war years thus find the chickens, the rabbits and the family pig feeding the League of Nations.

Cornish by name and Cornish by nature not only do I now have two Mums and Dads and two loving families, but I have also gone plural in

George's father, Charlie Cornish on his rounds as an employee of Keat & Sons, Bude.
Photo Cornish/Hemmerle family archive.

speech. There is a significantly different vernacular between Kings Hill and Belle Vue. A whole new vocabulary, dialect, accent and expression is available to me in Marina and I quickly absorb this. Both Teddy and I find ourselves in difficulty and for different reasons. Teddy's already accomplished command of the English language is not founded on Cornish expressions. 'Did 'e pushbike up 'ere? 'No, I rode my bike'.

Back in Belle Vue and I am chastised by Mum. I stoutly defend my right and heritage and protest 'But I don't want to speak proper'. For both Teddy and Bertram, foreign nationals, there is a whole new meaning to the word 'abroad'. Not only are upcountry people 'furriners' but the word 'abroad' has wide currency. A relationship that is not prospering has 'falled abroad'. A point of view that is not shared is ' all abroad in its thinking'. A wall that has been demolished has been 'scat abroad'.

Next door to Marina is 104 Kings Hill occupied by Charles McCandless and his wife Min, well Aunty Min to be precise, as she is sister of George Cornish's mother, long departed. Charles had been a Royal Navy destroyer Captain in the first world war, the destroyer having been sunk by a German U boat in the Mediterranean. In World War Two he was the local ARP warden and went around on the most

Micky and Gertie Cornish (left) with Mary and Bertram Glibert with their identical motorbikes on Marina front lawn.

Photo Cornish/Hemmerle family archive

extraordinary contraption of a pedal cycle with a small fuel tank loaded to the cross bar feeding an engine attached to the rear wheel for going up hills.

Charles, or Charmac as he is affectionately known by the family, feeds Micky's enthusiasm for motor bikes, lending the money for each new bike to be paid back in instalments by Micky from his weekly wage packet. On a trip to Barnstaple to pick up a new motor bike with Charmac driving his Austin Eight they hit the ice and end up in a ditch which puts Charmac in Stratton Hospital. Micky smuggles in his baccy and gets a strong rebuke from Matron.

In retaliation Charmac establishes a combative relationship with Matron demanding her attendance to hear his complaint that not enough butter was spread on his bread at tea time. Drawing herself to full height Matron informs him firmly she has indeed herself buttered the bread. 'In that event' replied Charmac 'would she investigate as to who scraped if off?'

Charles is fastidious in maintaining his naval traditions. An

35

eccentric in his habits, funded by the sale of 18 houses he had inherited in Northern Ireland the proceeds from the sale of which he kept in his current account - to his mind away from the prying eyes of the tax man. Every evening sees him cycling down Kings Hill to Bude and the Conservative Club for his Navy rum, returning for his evening meal which Min is required to deliver to precise time and place. After this he moves to the front room overlooking Kings Hill to smoke his pipe. Should it be that Min is in the orchard at the bottom of their back garden or in conversation with the Cornish family, he stands at the back porch of the house and hollers out into the garden ... 'Min - your place is in the kitchen'. Charmac eventually goes doolally.

III

Bude
Primary School

The River Neet immediately below Nanny Moores Bridge with Bude Recreation Ground from the Grenville Hotel with the Shalder Hills and Bude Primary School beyond.

Photo the Adrian Abbott collection

Footpath through the Shalder Hills to Bude Primary School, with Bude Canal and Branch Railway line beyond.

Photo the Adrian Abbott collection

The time has come for Jon Ball to start at school. As one of the post war bulge I am not short of class mates when joining Mrs Yelland's form dressed in short grey trousers, elastic belt with S fastener on the front, Start Rite brown sandals, shirt and a sleeveless Fair Isle jumper.

The journey to school from 18 The Strand is but a few minutes walk including dawdling time. Emerging from the alley way we cross The Strand and follow the river as it flows to the sea, left over Nanny Moores Bridge, past Paddy Frost's front door to the Shalder Hills sand dunes through which a footpath snakes to the school back door and an area where our mums congregate to exchange gossip, the big moments of small Bude's day.

School life at Bude Church of England Voluntary Primary School

Nanny Moores Bridge. The journey to and from school could be hazardous.
Photo the Adrian Abbott collection

is stern. The Victorian vernacular building first accommodates the almost overwhelming authoritative presence of Headmaster Hedley Luke presiding with a demeanour that would frighten a police horse. Bespectacled, dapper, tweed suited with sleeveless Fair Isle jumper, he rules with the cane across the palm of our hands. He has a passion for the elementary education of those of us in his charge. He is to be feared but we all share a sense of fairness, with Mum and Dad content seeing his superintendence a severe virtue.

Each week we have a visit from the Rev Walter Prest, incumbent at St Michael and All Angels. Walter Prest is a chum of Dad's and fellow founder of Bude Rotary Club. I look forward to his weekly pastoral visits as on the occasions that he comes into our classroom and we exchange glances, I get a wink.

We are in the gentle caring hands of Mrs Yelland. Her and our classroom is on the front south facing elevation adjacent to Bude Canal, looking towards Petherick's coal yard behind the high sandstone wall. Not that we can see much. The Victorian stern purposeful architecture is designed with high window sills and splayed reveals to let the light in but not allowing those inside to see outside. Dolly daydreamers cannot see much more than sky and clouds skittering along wafted by breezy Bude prevailing winds that have travelled all the way across the Atlantic to be with us. The Atlantic ocean is regularly referred to when we are asked to envisage gigantic space.

The fact that we cannot see out of the windows does not insulate us from the external sounds that so define the memories of our days in Mrs Yelland's classroom. Sounds gentle and reassuring, sounds consistent with the substantial tranquillity of our coastal community with its slow pace of life and progress in post war Britain. Sounds define this happy, innocent characteristic. A place where small things have big consequences and small events such as going to the pictures take on a huge significance in our lives.

The clip clop of the horses' hooves being led past our front playground always paint pictures in our minds of the canal side forge. It is the first building landwards from the Atlantic tidal lock gates where the canal meets Summerleaze beach. It's a place where we often linger to watch the sparks flying like a flock of starlings through operation of the ancient leather bellows. We all have miniature lucky horse shoes as keepsakes from the blacksmith Mr Staddon in exchange for our thrupenny bits.

Mr Staddon looks to us to be of a Biblical age, a timeline frontier, standing there next to the anvil as if an altar to his calling. He is wiry and muscular with his heavy, well worn leather apron tied at the front and stained where the horse's hoof rests on his thighs with his knees bent gently. Unlike the patient, well behaved horses time is surely no longer standing still for this Bude anachronism. Haste is seldom seen in Bude and, indeed, to many of the local populace, is unknown. Fred Staddon is the epitome of this.

Each morning there is the toot, toot of the steam train clanking its way from Bude station down the wharf branch line to Petherick's coal wharf and passing across the road just before Falcon Bridge and only a few yards from our classroom window. It runs along between Bude marshes and parallel to the canal tow path. There is a prominent sign with white letters on a big black background 'Catch Points' and it is here the steam train stops. The shunter alights, opens the gate, holds up the traffic and the driver, that one day we all hope to follow, applies the steam. Visitors to the town gather to watch what is a fascination for

Holding up the traffic at Falcon Bridge 1960.

Photo the Adrian Abbott collection

young and old alike.

But it is the less leisurely, more earnest sounds that always arrest our attention and imagination. The fire siren is located on top of the South

43

Western Electricity Board roof behind and above the Carriers Inn. Its air raid duties over the siren now musters Bude's retained firemen in times of need who rush to the fire station next door to our school. In our heads, we secretly count how much time passes from when we hear the siren to when we hear the bells of the fire engine mounted on the front bumper when it passes our front playground.

After dark the firemen are summoned by night bells. George Cornish is a fireman. He has a cast bell wired into Marina and mounted at high level on a mahogany board with a large striker. When Corky and George's room is on a B&B let in the summer Corky jams a rolled up pair of George's socks between the bell and striker to ensure her summer visitors are not frightened out of their lives by its clamour.

The whoosh of the coastguard maroon if the rocket brigade and cliff rescue team is needed is one event that even interrupts our teaching.

Guardians of the town. The Bude Fire Brigade, post war.

Photo Bude Fire Brigade

The maroon is a loud retort and it signals distress, but it also sends other signals. It says 'Watch out!' as the coastguards rush to their trained assistance. It tells those in peril help is on the way. But most of all it says that we, the people of Bude, care and will do our utmost to help if wind, tide or storm have conspired with our Atlantic lee shore to place you in mortal danger. Also, as is pointed out to us, it sends hope. Hope beats faith and charity every time.

We all have vivid snapshots firmly imprinted in our consciousness from our earliest memories. Mine? A lesson for life at a tender age and this lesson is delivered on The Strand directly opposite Behenna's Garage adjacent to the riverside promenading pavement which gives meaning to the name of the street on which we live. It is - motor cars can also be dangerous things. That is why the front bumper is called the front bumper.

With carefree abandon I have stepped off the pavement with eyes firmly fixed on London House, a confectionary shop, near Behenna's Garage. I have gob stoppers in the front of my mind, a farthing each, four for a penny. The hazards of crossing a road are not even in my consciousness. I am hit four-square by the bumper of a Wolsey car on my flank. I am knocked unconscious. Quite a kerfuffle takes place with me soon opening my eyes and looking up to all these faces peering down at me, sprawled on the tarmacadam. Among the friendly, concerned eyes is someone who proudly announces his recent success in examination by the Bude Stratton Branch of the St John Ambulance Brigade as a volunteer. My ensuing physical examination confirms I am in the land of the living, hurt but substantially unharmed.

'This is young Jonny Ball from Wroes. His Mum and Dad will be in the shop just further along' and with that I am lifted up and carried horizontally in someone's arms along The Strand and into Wroes Ladies Outfitters. The summoned doctor arrives soon after and I am introduced to Dr Percy Corser who is new to the town. He soon secures the Ball family to his patients' list.

I have survived - no great harm done; Mum's panic is over and her relief expressed by eulogising what a charming doctor Percy is and what a great new asset he will be to the town - notwithstanding his frayed cuffs, observes Mum with her ever alert outfitter's eye. This is not the first occasion along The Strand where I survive a near death experience.

The Ball family are not regular churchgoers and after working for a

Bude Sea Pool c1950 with brother Chris and sister Jenny.

Photo Ball family archive

solid six days Sundays have the air of precious. A Sunday outing to the pub or tending our small garden up the Delabole slate steps to the rear where Mum hangs out the washing is not a culture or habit handed down to us. If we are not on an expedition in the Ford Pop Sunday is a day when the time passes quietly and simply. Dad likes a relaxing Sunday afternoon bath and us children are encouraged to be out in the fresh air. A favourite pastime is feeding the ducks on the River Neet, a simple pleasure that from the earliest age I find both fascinating and absorbing, even from within my pram.

Alas one Sunday afternoon, in my enthusiasm I forget to let go of the bread and fall from my pram through a gap in the tamarisk hedge into the river Neet. We are only yards from our front door. Brother Chris jumps into the river to save me; sister Jenny rushes home with the startling news that I am drowning to dear Dad sat in the bath cutting his toenails.

Poor Jenny pays a heavy price for bringing panic to the Sunday afternoon quiet. She is given a sharp smack for not looking after me well enough and is sent to bed. In time yet to be this injustice does not diminish and is a story that is told time and time again. My survival at the hands of my siblings is destined to be an occurrence that none of us forget and figures in endless permutations of interpretation when matters of fairness and equity are topics of family conversation.

It is the summer of 1953. King George VI has died the previous year whilst Princess Elizabeth is up a tree in Kenya and this event has heralded great change. Everything from stamps to post boxes, to coinage, official documents hitherto embossed with GR V1 gives way to E11R. The impending Coronation is the topic of conversation on everyone's

Bude
School
Nineteen fifty three

School photograph to celebrate the Cornonation June 1953.
Photo Ball family Archive.

lips throughout the land and indeed what remains of the British Empire. Those are the bits coloured pink on the large grained map of the world prominently hung on the classroom wall. Mrs Short, our teacher, explains it is already a bit out of date. We are the post war bulge. There are 46 of us in our form at Bude Church of England Voluntary Primary School so it's a good job that discipline is the watchword. We all have our photographs taken to celebrate the Coronation.

Alas this great State occasion is destined to secure a different memory for me. I have succumbed to chicken pox and all the jollity and celebrations come and go with me in bed. How unfair is that. I miss the planned street parties with the bunting and the Union flags. It rains and rains and I watch the rain drops bouncing, or are they dancing, on and off the lead flat roof outside the glazed French doors - my bedroom window to the world.

My own patriotic flag on a long lollypop stick is there on the bed with me nearly too feeble to wave it and feeling very sorry for myself. Despite the rain there is so much going on and I am missing it all. Even standing on the bed I cannot see over the parapet of the flat roof. And to make matters worse I suddenly hear the loud 'Boom' of the canons, the historic canons owned by Chips Petvin, brought out of their long retirement in order to deliver a Coronation Salute. Her Majesty Queen Elizabeth II is to be left in no doubt that her loyal subjects in Bude are engaging wholeheartedly in our version of pomp and pageantry to record this important moment in all our lives. Bude has a remoteness in place and time, the end of the line metaphorically and actually. Next stop the Atlantic Ocean, then the Falkland Islands. A long way in every sense, sight and mind, from the policy agenda papers of Cornwall County Hall Truro, let alone from the red Ministerial boxes of Whitehall. We are treated as an outpost of Empire and Coronation Day 1953 might pass with Bude unseen but, thanks to Chips Petvin, certainly not with Bude

The first up-train of the morning due to depart.

Photo The Adrian Abbott Collection.

unheard.

Up the stairs comes Mum with a present in her hand for me. The kindly dinner ladies from school who have prepared the Coronation tea treat have looked into the shop on their way home with my share of the tea. These treats are brought up in an empty Spillers Red Ring Flour bag. In post war Bude nothing is thrown out.

And so whilst Paddy and one or two other classmates have televisions at home to view this great State occasion, the thought that we might also have a television is still light years away from entering Dad's consciousness. It is gathering round the wireless for us. I think it is Aunty Win who gives brother Chris a magnificent miniature gilded cast metal Coronation coach with horses and out riders. It is our most enduring emblem of what is going on in far away London and we queue up to take it in turns to move Her Majesty across the carpet in our first floor sitting room in her metal cast state finery with 'Empire Made' stamped on the underside of the coach.

I don't think there is any boy in my class who doesn't want to be an engine driver when we grow up. From the Halt sign at the bottom of Kings Hill the steam trains are parallel to the road as far back as Bude Gas Works. Whenever I walk up to Corky's we linger to watch

Bude station frontage from the west with station master's house in the foreground.
Photo The Adrian Abbott Collection.

the shuntings, the watering, the coaling and operation of the turn table propelled by nothing more than the muscle of the shunter. It is dirty, it is noisy but never less than thrilling. Many school holiday hours are idled away observing and dreaming of our engine driving careers. We are not allowed onto the platform without buying a platform ticket - cost one penny, unless, that is, we are able to persuade Mr Reg Abbott that we've come to make a purchase from W H Smith's newspaper and book stall. Along with the Station Buffet this runs the length of the station platform between the Booking Hall and the Station Master's house at the west end of the platform.

Paddy starts his morning newspaper round from here at crack of dawn. Paddy is friends with David Moss who runs the book stall at W H Smith's. The papers are sorted having arrived on the first down train of the day and Paddy loads his bike for the first of his two rounds before school. David also puts aside a single copy of the Western Morning News folded and held with an elastic band to hand to the guard of the morning up train of the day.

From Bude the first station is Whitstone and Bridgerule and en route the train puffs its way up the rising hinterland and through the front garden of Trelay farmed by Micky and Angie Grills. They own a spaniel which has been trained for special duty each morning. As the train passes through the front garden of Trelay by the farmhouse, the guard tosses the Western Morning News across onto the front lawn where the waiting spaniel retrieves the paper to take it to his master and the breakfast table following the morning milking of the cows. This splendid arrangement becomes a real canine challenge on Fridays, the day Farmers' Weekly comes out.

Bude station, which holds so much interest for us is, at this hour of our lives, the main gateway to the town. The railway is an important method of transport, sometimes the only method of transport available. There are motor cars, but not that many and the supremacy of the railway still rules. It is rare a day passes without talk of the war or its impact on our town and the lives of older schoolchildren who have left Bude Primary for Bude Grammar School or Stratton Secondary Modern. Stories are told of evacuees arriving at the start of the war and, indeed, troop carrying trains are still with us with National Servicemen arriving and departing for gunnery practice at Cleave Camp.

Famously something happens in the summer that attracts a sizeable number of us to await the arrival of a special rain. This train carries the circus, greeted with a hubbub of expectation. We have elephants in Bude. They arrive in converted cattle wagons especially strengthened for this purpose and, leaving the station, parade down Bencoolen Road and along The Strand trunk to tail. At the bus stop the elephant keeper leads them down into the middle of the river in front of the Central Methodist Church their compensation and reward for forbearance during their train journey.

Circus elephants in the river Neet having paraded down The Strand.

Photo the Adrian Abbott collection

50

Boating on the River Neet. The Strand Bude, c1956.

Photo the Adrian Abbott collection

And it is not only arrivals that capture our interest at the station. The mid afternoon departure from Bude, the 3.15, is the focus each day for all local farmers, fishermen, growers and producers to despatch their produce to city markets far away. This train, to many locals, is as famous as the Atlantic Coast Express which brings the visitors on whom so much the economy of the town depends and just five hours from London Waterloo. But the 3.15 up train is held in similar affection. It is called 'The Perisher' on account of the mainstay of its purpose, the conveyance of perishables. A Perisher has also left at five past three from Padstow with meat, fish and flowers, all London bound, meeting with the Bude train at Halwill Junction before transfer on to London Nine Elms.

Life in Bude is very much living and eating with the seasons. There must be four or five greengrocers scattered around the town centre, but our favourite is Charlie Clowes two thirds of the way up Belle Vue, on the right hand side with all his fruit and vegetables displayed on gently sloping pallets with the prices handsomely written in each section facing outwards to the customer. This spills onto Belle Vue and the shop is a constant hubbub of activity throughout the mornings.

It is also a bazaar where bartering takes place. Corky comes into town with her imitation brown snakeskin bag with its large handles with all her surplus runner beans and exchanges them with Charlie Clowes for produce that she does not grow.

The first early new potatoes of the season are keenly anticipated. The very first crop to be pulled all come from a few miles down the coast, grown on the steep, south facing sunny slopes of the valleys at Boscastle. This unique topography provides a good source of income for the village in the post war years. Charlie proudly displays the first of the season under the handwritten tag of 'Boscastles'. It is quite some years later when I have left Bude Primary School and am a Boarder at Truro School before I am to understand that all new potatoes do not come from Boscastle.

Mum and Dad are firm in their view that we only spend our pocket money in the town and in shops where local families are the proprietors. We are banned from going into the Co-op and the illicit thrill of one day entering this shop at the top of the town on Corky's hand lingers a long time. Equally, we, the Ball family, do not hold strong political views; politics is not a meal time topic and as for local and party politics generally this is a matter upon which Dad is robust. Politics is a luxury we, as a shop keeping family, cannot afford. The customer is King, or more precisely, Queen.

Buses and trains are certainly a central interest in our young lives and our town's economy in equal measure and with the Southern National bus garage next door to us at 18 The Strand these things are never far from sight or mind. It was to this bus office next door that Mum has gone on 3rd June 1947 seeking advice as to the bumpiest ride on offer from and returning to The Strand. I spend my last hours in utero bouncing up and down in Mum's tummy on the coast road to Crackington Haven travelling along some of the finest coastal scenery anywhere in the world whether it is coloured pink on the map of the world or not. Thanks to Southern National and Mum's ingenuity the 4th June 1947 sees me entering the world in sunny Bude weighing in at more than 9 lbs. This immediately secures me the nickname of Joe Baski after the heavyweight boxing champion of the day.

In Bude Thursday is early closing and throughout the summer on Thursdays we have the Furry dances around the streets with Bude Town Band. We all congregate by the Triangle with its fountain erected to commemorate the Coronation of King Edward and us schoolchildren are dragooned into this evening procession with which we entertain our

Anderton and Rowland September fair on the lower wharf Bude canal. Aerial view from Bude Castle hill.

Photo The Adrian Abbott Collection.

visitors to the town and celebrate our Cornish cultural heritage.

We are marshalled by old Mr Aunger, a lifelong devotee of the town band, and both his sons Ken and Derek are ardent bandsmen. Derek is in the same form as me at Primary School. In front of Mr Bartrop's wireless and electrical shop we perform the Floral dance in groups of eight, four plus four and each week Mr Aunger reminds us, not that we need it, the steps we must perform as he explains this Cornish curiosity to our visitors encouraging their own children to join in along with us.

Mr Aunger is heard above the congregating hubbub because he has a loud voice and because he uses an ancient hand held megaphone, surely as old as he is, battered and dented to match and be in tune with the older tuba instruments that make up the band.

Each week we oompaah up Belle Vue and down Queen Street, past the bottom of Kings Street and then down Lansdown Road and along The Strand ending by Falcon Bridge and in front of the Falcon Inn. Here we all join hands in a circle for the finale where the final rounds of

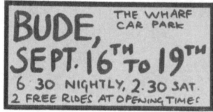

The Anderton and Rowlands September Fair. One of the highlights of our year. Original poster Nigel Vanstone.

the Floral Dance are delivered at a ferocious pace, as we wheel round faster and faster, whooping and giddy.

We assume this fun-packed finale takes place on this open space for our benefit. In truth, our evening is ended adjacent to the front lawn of the Falcon Inn and as we take our parents' hands for home and bed, the bandsmen head into the pub. The Falcon Inn is famous for its landlord, Des Gregory, pulling the pints and dishing up the abuse for which he is legendary. With September comes the last of the season's furry dances, the week before one of the most eagerly awaited events of the year - the arrival of Bude Fair. Anderton and Rowlands have brought their travelling fair here for as long as anyone can remember and we are in the heydays of this institution. The fair is erected on the Lower Wharf next to the canal and stretches all the way back to Nanny Moores Bridge in front of Bude Castle and the entire length of the Bude Recreation Ground.

Immediately in front of the Castle grounds is the boxing ring which is Dad's favourite and the number one sport of his early years. He had narrowly lost on points as losing finalist in a west country amateur light weight championships in 1926, to a Scotsman. But this achievement had seen him, for a short time, elevated to a position on the West of England Boxing Board of Control, only relinquished prior to his move to Bude.

We have our local hero Ted Hamley who had been a boxing champion during his time in the Royal Navy. This always assures a large crowd. The boxing ring is owned and run by Sam and Esther McKeowen. Sam is renowned for the way he whips up his trade with his own fairground boxers paraded before us with the banter flying and fear lurking in their eyes knowing the local boy has never been beaten.

Just along from the boxing ring is the smartest fairground caravan of them all. This belongs to Mrs DeVey. It is spotless in every way and is a trailer which has been located in prime position for surveillance and amenity for its proprietorial owner. Special outside travelling steps give access to the front door with gleaming stainless steel water containers either side as if ceremonial urns giving presence and dignity to the entrance way into what I think to be an Aladdin's cave. For Mum and Dad it is the hall of audience.

It is not only gleaming from the outside it is also magnificent on the inside and I know this. I have been inside. I have sat down. I have been entertained with lemonade whilst Mum and Dad take tea. Mrs DeVey is one of Mum's valued customers. Mum and Dad share my delight when September comes around. Mum knows Mrs DeVey's garments of choice and the stock will be there waiting her arrival and her stroll along The Strand to peruse the garments She brings no money with her to the shop. She returns to her caravan unburdened with her purchases, all this being the protocol established between fairground proprietor and local shop keeper. No doubt the Ball family are not alone in such time honoured traditions.

It is early evening and I am off to the fair with Mum and Dad. Along The Strand, over Nanny Moores Bridge, past the Houdini-like character adjacent to the gates into the Recreation Ground, sat there amongst chains, giant padlocks, and large hessian sacks and dividing his Bude time between giving his shows and spending his rewards at the Carriers' Inn just along from us in The Strand. We do not dally as Dad has bags on each hand. Both Mum and Dad are smartly dressed. At the caravan steps Dad adjusts his tie, knocks and we are cordially invited to enter.

The new purchases are reviewed and discussed, compliments are exchanged. I am mesmerised by the beautifully etched glass and interior befitting a master craftsman born with a showman's eye. Just before we leave the final part of the transaction takes place. From underneath banquette seating behind a small panelled door is brought a galvanised bucket which is handed to Dad. We depart,me hand in hand with Mum onward to the fair. Dad returns, past Houdini, over Nanny Moores Bridge back to 18 the Strand. He carries with him the bucket full of thrupenny bits, angular and twelve sided, many with the head of the King, some with the new Queen, four to the shilling and eighty to the pound.

Nanny Moores Bridge on a spring flood tide with Paddy's House still getting a battering.
Photo the Adrian Abbott collection

Bude Fair Week in September is a time in our year when our lively minds are fed the fantastical. It is the month when we move up a form in the new school year with a different teacher and a new classroom. Alongside this with the fair we see and experience things outside our regular and regulated lives. How does the Houdini man get out of his padlocked chains inside the hessian sack? The Big Wheel gives us birds-eye views completely distorting our so-well-known landscape surrounding school and canal side. The Hall of Mirrors suspends reality and depicts us as unreal. The motor cyclists on the Wall of Death put our understanding of the concept of gravity on strike. The knife throwing act has knife thrower and target both dressed in wild west apparel and feathered headdresses. They are straight out of the films at Bude Picture House. We watch in mesmerised suspense.

Each September Anderton and Rowlands weave their magical spell to enchant and fascinate; the bindings to our shared end of summer childhood memories.

Paddy Frost lives with his Mum and Dad at 1 Leven Cottages. Its gable wall is immediately next to Nanny Moores bridge and incorporated into the river bank. Sandbags play a big part in Paddy's life. His house and back garden regularly floods. Leven Cottages are probably the lowest lying of all residences hereabouts, along with The Crescent where all residents accept regular flooding as a fact of life.

Paddy's Dad, Eddie Frost, known as Jack to all his workmates, is chums with Dad. They go off on trips to Plymouth in our Ford Pop to watch Plymouth Argyle play football. The Frosts don't own a motor car, we do. The Frosts do own a television, we don't. It is some time before this is to change.

Jean and Teddy live in a flat in Belle Vue over the Duchy Bakeries shop owned by the Parsons brothers, not far from us along The Strand. The Parsons family has a benevolent approach to all employees. The Duchy Bakery flat has a long steep stairway and the main living accommodation overlooks Belle Vue and the Triangle where Mr Aunger musters us with his megaphone for furry dances around the town on a Thursday. Hot water to Jean and Teddy's flat is provided via an ancient gas geyser in the kitchen area. It is temperamental and untrustworthy. The ever resourceful Teddy looks to history for his inspired safeguard against the serious hazards that might attach to malfunction of the geyser.

A third occupant becomes resident above the Duchy Bakery shop - a melodious canary, a happy bird, christened Sweetie Pie, who merrily chirps away the days in tune with the music on the wireless. Sweetie Pie is a joyful addition to the household. Whenever the gas geyser thunders into life a watchful eye is kept on Sweetie Pie. On several occasions the tweet, tweeting stops and there is Sweetie Pie laid out on the floor of the cage whereupon the gas geyser is shut down, the windows opened to ventilate the flat and we all go out onto the flat roof and to Atlantic breezes along with Sweetie Pie who is soon restored to perch and song.

Sister Jenny who only occasionally joins me on my regular visits here is also soon to acquire a canary. She wins one at Anderton and Rowlands September fair. Mum and Dad are not best pleased that we have another resident at 18 The Strand. The temporary cardboard box with holes for it to breathe through is replaced by a proper cage the next day purchased by Dad at the pet shop up in the town. Jenny's weekly pocket money is six pence and Dad, ever keen to have us appreciate the value of money, sequestrates Jenny's weekly pocket money for instalment repayment of the cage. But alas within the shortest while, we are up the back Delabole slate steps to our small rear garden where Mum hangs out the washing to conduct a short service and to bury the canary. For countless weeks after poor Jenny gazes at the empty canary cage in the corner, all forlorn, whilst continuing to be denied her pocket money until the cage is paid off.

The only exposure to any other sort of culture is The Picture House, Bude's dream palace, at the top of the town. This is the largest covered space locally for public congregation and is well known for its splendid Art Deco foyer, as close as Bude gets to putting on the Ritz .We have regular family mid week visits. We always sit upstairs in the Balcony, and watch suitable Hollywood Musicals or Western movies and Ealing Studio delights. The billing also includes Pearl and Dean advertisements and Pathé News which is the only time we experience images attached to the spoken word on world events.

At the end of each evening performance the National Anthem is played. The house lights go up and we all stand to attention whilst an image of the Royal Standard fluttering in the breeze over Buckingham Palace is projected onto the screen. As far as I know none of us at Bude Primary School has ever been to London, let alone seen the changing of the guard at Buckingham Palace. Departing Bude Picture House I am part of the largest crowd of people I ever experience beyond those occasions when Dad takes me to watch Plymouth Argyle playing football. We make haste down Belle Vue to get in Jan Darch's fish and chip shop queue for our final homeward treat.

In the years immediately following the 1953 Coronation the greatest event of any moment to us is the end of rationing in the summer of 1954. Another of Dad's business chums, Mr Norman Abbott, runs a sweet shop in Belle Vue. Without a ration coupon we are lost, except for one occasion. Neither Mum nor Corky can believe it as I am never lost for a word, but Dr Percy Corser diagnoses that I am tongue-tied. I will need to submit to a procedure of having a snip underneath my tongue which must take place without anaesthetic. Next door to the library in the bowels of Bude Castle, Cornwall County Council operates a unit for a visiting medical officer in charge of the welfare of schoolchildren. Corky takes me to see him and the decision is made. He will operate there and then.

I am not sure which is worse, the pain or having mouthfuls of blood that will not stem. Corky hurries me back across Nanny Moores Bridge and up to Abbotts sweet shop. No she doesn't have any coupons, but look at the poor boy. I have blood dribbling down my chin and tears streaming down my face. The well of human kindness clicks in and I am rewarded with a bar of Fry's chocolate. We stand outside on the pavement in Belle Vue with Corky cuddling me and there am I on my way to additional comfort from Mum with my Fair Isle sleeveless jumper covered in blood and chocolate.

This is life in rural north Cornwall. The medicine of the time is consistent with the privations of the age, but the caring in the community is never found wanting. As for culture, this can perhaps break down between the indoors and the outdoors. Our school books introduce us to art and literature but opera or ballet completely pass us by. The Bude Picture House gives us occasional glimpses of life in America which is indeed very different to our own. The youth of America are storming the barricades of conformity, way beyond our wildest horizons. It is to the outdoors that we look for our cultural development.

IV

The Winds Call No Man Sir

Bude vessel Traly in the lock gates c1946, her last year of service. In the background is the tarred hobblers' hut. Seaborne trade rarely entered Bude harbour without assistance from the hobblers in small open row-boats. The hobblers were unlicensed pilots making fast the ropes from the ships to the buoys and booms marking the channel, allowing the crews to warp their vessels up to the lock gates.

Photo the Adrian Abbott collection

... A deeper import for ever lurks in the legends told to us in our infant years than lies upon the truth we live to learn ...

Samuel Taylor Coleridge 1772 - 1834

It is the treasures of landscape, fine surf beaches aplenty and majestic cliff walks which feed my imagination ... we certainly have legends and saints galore, back to the Venerable Bede living on Chapel Rock, halfway along the Breakwater, through to the eccentric Victorian Parson, Robert Stephen Hawker of Morwenstow. Hawker's poetry and prose define my local landscape and its people. His writings forever give him association similar to that enjoyed between Thomas Hardy and Dorset or Wordsworth and the Lake District. His devotion has left wild Morwenstow a better place. He was a man who shone with his times. Most importantly, perhaps, it was 'Passon Hawker' that gave the Cornish our Anthem to Celtic Nationhood, *'And Shall Trelawny live, And shall Trelawny die, Here's 20,000 Cornishmen shall know the reason why.'* Written under Sir Bevil Grenville's great oak in Stowe woods The Song of the Western Men harvests belonging and patriotic fervour, leaving Cornishmen the world over in thraldom for the land of their birth.

How to describe this landscape of my youth? It is wildness. It is a remote loneliness. It is inaccessibility. It is governance of and by the seasons. Most of all it is the wind and the lash of the Atlantic gales that define Bude's spirit of place, our genius loci. The precipitous cliffs stand defiant. Beyond this the hedgerows and trees all subordinate; they crouch, they genuflect, they contort to the prevailing weather, even mighty oaks are stunted. Nothing organic abounding is unresponsive to these higher orders. The winds call no man Sir. They waft the clouds which obscure the sun. Without wind to shift the clouds the stars no longer shine.

When I say 'loneliness' it should not be thought of in any melancholy sense, to the contrary in fact. The local inhabitants are at one with their weather beaten surroundings. Human toil and dignified endeavour have transformed only some coastal land to productive use. Much remains wild, unaltered and buffeted by elements demented. Cornwall will forever be a stronghold for Mother Nature, with the Cornish people handmaidens to her story and her ways.

We are born to this wild, wind and sea-shaped geography which in turn shapes us, inclining us to its will, bending our minds to nature's laws. We are constantly connecting to our coastal environment. The saints, the myths, the legends and the sense of belonging feed the dreaming of our dreams. Plenty of dream time takes place on Summerleaze where natural forces certainly hold sway. The sand freshly upholstered with each tide, the salt winds not to breathe but to inhale and sunsets so, so special as light surrenders day.

Summerleaze Beach, stretches landwards to Bude Castle and the Shalder Hills sand dunes nearly up to Nanny Moores Bridge, the playground of my youth. The magic is in the not quite knowing where nature stops and manmade starts. The summer time gaiety, cheerfulness, colour and just having fun. It is where the River Neet, beside the tamarisk-lined Strand, flows to the sea. It is the wild and wide horizons and the westward boundary of my known world. Within the high gothic of the towering cliffs with their mnemonic vertical stratification,

'They came in paths of storm, they found,
This quiet home in Christian ground.'

Figurehead of the Caledonia (wrecked in 1842) in Morwenstow churchyard. It marks the grave of Captain and crew. Behind and adjacent to the lytch gate the granite Celtic cross with inscription ..'To the Glory of God, and in memory of shipwrecked sailors buried in this graveyard unknown and yet well known. He sent from on high, He took me, He drew me out of great waters'.

Photo Dr Bob Willingham

Summerleaze is our cathedral to curiosity where we pass so many idle hours in our young lives.

In winter months that which wind and tide have brought to shore is our inheritance as much as our fascination. Our soon erased footprints are following in the footsteps of a generational tradition. On the south head to the canal lock gates, opened for seaborne trade to secure safe harbour within the canal lower basin, is the ancient tarred hobblers' hut. It is where the old Bude men of the sea gather to smoke their pipes, reminisce, foretell and enthral my generation with their stories of Bude in the olden days. They tell of that which came ashore in their days. It helped build the houses we live in. It gave names to our streets, our bridges and our meadows. It was a bounteous cargo of consumables heaven sent to Bude during the rationed war years. For the length of their own memories and generations before it added to the gravestones in our churchyards. It prompted R S Hawker's 1842 stirring words beneath the figure-head of the Caledonia at her captain's grave:

We laid them in their lowly rest,
The strangers of a distant shore;
We smoothed the green turf on their breast,
'Mid baffled Ocean's angry roar,
And there, the relique of the storm,
We fixed fair Scotland's figured form

She watches by her bold, her brave
Her shield towards the fatal sea
Their cherished lady of the wave
Is guardian of their memory
Stern is her look, but calm for there
No gale can bend or billow bear

Stand, silent image! stately stand
Where sighs shall breathe and tears be shed
And many a heart of Cornish land
Will soften for the stranger dead.
They came in paths of storm, they found
This quiet home in Christian ground.

Robert Stephen Hawker
1803 -1875

This landscape of rural north Cornwall has amassed memories and memorials to Cornwall's history. We Cornish are a loyal lot when it comes to the past. We take time for change to take a welcome hold – 'us 'ave to belong to doing it.' So it has been down the centuries.

In 1497 Michael an Gof and Thomas Flamank led the Cornish Rebellion in protest at King Henry V11's penal taxes levied to pay for an invasion of Scotland. The Cornish army marched on London and to defeat at the Battle of Blackheath. This Cornish army was the last to raise arms, march on London and actually get there. The leaders were both hanged, drawn and quartered but as an Gof went to his Maker he proclaimed he would have ' a name perpetual and a fame permanent and immortal'. And so it has been these five hundred years.

With the 16th century came Henry V111 and his Papal discontent that disturbed by his decree the people's solemn relationship with God, so set in its ways hereabouts. With the new King Edward V1 in 1547 came the abolition of the well loved Prayer Book together with many church festivals. These times, four hundred years before my own, were tumultuous indeed for my forebears on this land. Once again, the Cornish rose in arms and rebellion. They marched under the leadership of Sir Humphrey Arundell in the year 1549, until defeated at Exeter. They petitioned the King,

> 'We will not receyve the new Service, but we wyll have our olde Service of Mattens, masse, evensong and procession, in Latten, as it was before. And we the Cornyshe men, whereof certain of us understande no Englyshe, utterly refuse thys newe Service.'

Here proof indeed as to the Celtic language of Cornwall holding its ground. But unlike the Welsh it was not to be that the enforced new English Prayer Book was translated into the Celtic tongue of the far south west. These years of discontent grumbled on with the ways of the Reformation taking huge toll on altars and shrines, feasts and fairs and all accoutrements of the religious ways of Cornish life. It interfered with the way 'us Cornish is praisin' God.'

Within the span of a man's life came the English Civil War. Cornwall was always going to be for the King. Stratton saw a defining battle at Stamford Hill. The Cornish Royalist Army was led into battle by Sir

The surviving fortifications at Stowe Barton with Coombe Valley beyond and Cleave Camp in the distance. Evidence of the power of the prevailing wind abounds.

Photo Dr Bob Willingham

Bevil Grenville of Stowe on 16th May 1643. The great house of Stowe, no longer standing, was just five miles north of the field of battle. In the wooded Stowe valley and adjacent to the self same oak under which Hawker wrote his Cornish Anthem it is less than a mile from Duckpool and the birthday treats of my early days.

The English Civil War was of great moment in Cornwall. Following victory at Stratton the Cornish Army marched to Bath and the Battle of Lansdown Hill. Another Royalist victory, but at what cost to the Cornish? The bravest and noblest gentleman of Cornwall Sir Bevil Grenville fell in the service of his King despite the best efforts of his manservant Anthony Payne from Stratton, the Cornish Giant. He stood seven foot four inches and weighed 38 stone. His duty was to bring his master home. The faithful retainer wrote a letter to his lady at Stowe which survives.

'Honoured Madam

Ill news flieth apace. The heavy tidings no doubt hath already travelled to Stowe that we have lost our blessed Master by the enemy's advantage. You must not, dear Lady, grieve too much for your noble spouse ... his soul was in Heaven before his bones were cold. He fell as he often told us

67

Life-size copy of the painting of the Cornish Giant, Anthony Payne, which hangs in the courtyard of the Tree inn, Stratton. This is a copy of the original by Sir Godfery Kneller painted at the command of the king that hangs in the Royal Institution of Cornwall, Truro.

Photo Dr Bob Willingham

he wished to die ... for his country and his king. He delivered to me his last commands with such tender words for you and for his children as are not to be set down with my poor pen, but must come to your ears upon my best heart's breath ... Master John, when I mounted him on his father's horse, rode him into the war like a young prince, as he is, and our men followed him with swords drawn and with tears in their eyes. ... I am coming down with the mournfullest load that ever a poor servant did bear, to bring the great heart that is cold to Kilkhampton vault ... these, Honoured Madam, from thy saddest, truest Servant,

Anthony Payne'

A grateful King appointed Anthony Payne Governor of the Garrison at Plymouth with Royal appointment as Halberdier of the Guns. The King commanded his portrait to be painted by the Court artist Sir Godfrey Kneller and it hangs to this day in the Royal Institution of Cornwall. He returned to Stratton and died at The Tree Inn in 1691 in the very room wherein he was born.

In the words of Hawker ... 'after his death neither the door nor the stairs would afford egress for the large and coffined corpse. The joists had to be sawn through and the floor lowered with rope and pulley, to enable the giant to pass out towards his mighty grave. Relays of strong bier-men carried him to his rest, and the bells of Stratton Tower, by his own express desire, chimed him home. He was buried in a tomb outside the southern wall of Stratton Church.'

With the Restoration and Charles 11 on the throne, the title of Lord Stratton was bestowed on Sir John Berkeley who had fought under Grenville at the battle of Stamford Hill. Berkeley Square with the adjacent Stratton Street became a permanent memorial in the heart of London's Mayfair. Sir Bevil Grenville's son John becomes the first Earl of Bath. In Stratton church is the handsome 'Royal Coat of Arms' given by Charles 11 in tribute to those whose lives were delivered up in the Royalist cause. It is local testament to Stratton's moment of history in the life of our nation.

The story of Stratton and Strattonians has thus prospered and survives not least because of the civic importance of this settlement. Its roots go back a very long way indeed. Stratton is mentioned in the 901

The Tree Inn, Stratton formerly the Manor House whose origins precede Norman Times. It was the Royalist base for the battle of Stamford Hill and home to the Cornish Giant Anthony Payne.

Photo Dr Bob Willingham

Will of Alfred the Great, 185 years before the Doomsday book. From the time of Doomsday through to the 19th century Cornwall was divided for administrative purposes into 'Hundreds'. From their introduction Stratton was the only settlement in all Cornwall whose significance determined that the Hundred would bear its name.

In listening to the voices of our landscape there is no finer starting point in Cornwall than the parish churches. They are a pattern book of history in the way the local population run their lives, praise their God, erect their monuments and employ local materials in building for shelter and congregation. Here in north Cornwall they exemplify the spirit of each age. With Sir John Betjeman at St Enodoc and St Endellion, Thomas Hardy at St Juliot and Robert Stephen Hawker at St Morwenna and St John the Baptist the churches become the touch points for great writers.

It is the churches which hold the history, were vandalised by the Puritans and bore witness to the highs and the lows of the Christian faith as it journeyed through the centuries. This journey produced its heroes and none more heroic than John Wesley. With his brother Charles he brought the Methodist movement to the far south west. The Wesleyan ethos took firm hold and nonconformism flourished. Why wouldn't it? It was the very hearth and home of the Celt and the Celtic way of life.

Lay preaching spanned from high oratory to quaint. It offered ordering to lives, education to children and fear of God as a living force for good. Brass bands and choir singing were at the heart of both Chapel and community, a rich cultural expression that reinforced Cornwall's place in the world, its pride in its own nationhood and fed the Cornish Diaspora.

It was through the second half of the 19th century that Bude, breezy Bude, burgeoned from fuzzy down to flourishing town. It was seaside modern to Stratton ancient. Stratton remained the seat of justice with its Court House, and jealously guarded its traditions and status. Bude remained in Stratton's shadow. A sailor arriving in Bude in 1872 enquired as to a doctor in Bude. 'Well, Sir,' he was told, 'you see when the Quality's here in the summer us sends across to Stratton, but in winter us just dies a natural death.'

The Directors of the London and South Western Railway celebrated the opening of the final section of track from Holsworthy to Bude in August 1898. This line did not go through Stratton. The arrival of the

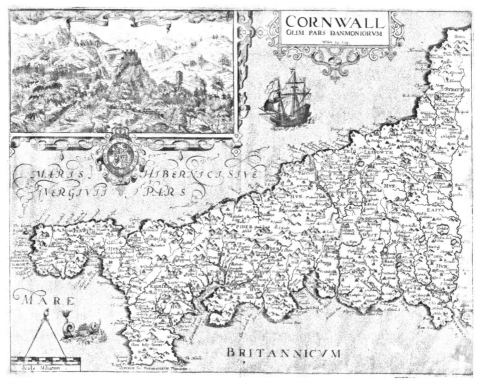

Map of Cornwall by William Kip 1607 showing Cornwall divided administratively into Hundreds. The Stratton Hundred covers the north-east Atlantic coastline of Cornwall. A millennium ago Stratton was only settlement in all Cornwall whose significance determined that the Hundred would bear its name

Map Ball family Archive

railway was the event that finally established Bude as the dominant settlement and put in place 'Stratton's gentle decline.' Notwithstanding it was to Stratton that Bude still looked for Cottage Hospital, the Alms Houses, the Union Poor House and the Police Station.

Unlike much of Cornwall the wealth of this area is not founded on mineral riches. It is the seaborne trade despite the cruel coastline that prospers and in turn gives way to the age of the visitor. By the end of the 19th century Cornwall's income deriving from copper and tin has dramatically declined. It is clear the economic future lay elsewhere. The Grenville Hotel in Bude follows shortly after the building of King Arthur's Castle Hotel at Tintagel and the Headland Hotel at Newquay, all responding to the significant increase of visitors to the area. In addition Bude sees a considerable rise in construction activity where guest houses and seaside dwellings are built. Sir Arthur Quiller Couch, Cornwall's most prominent man of letters of his age, captures the mood of the moment as Editor of the Cornish Magazine published in 1898. He opines,

'The suggestion is that Cornwall should turn her natural beauty to account and, by making it more widely known, at once benefit thousands and honestly enrich herself..... let us (cater for the stranger) do it well and honestly. Let us respect him and our native land as well.'

The spirit of the age, uniting with natural assets, sees Bude transforming itself into 'a first class watering place.' This sets the course for the town of my birth. No finer picture can be painted than that of the Atlantic Coast Express arriving in Bude. The journey took a little over five hours from London Waterloo and was heavily marketed by the railway company to ensure a return on their investment. These summer time express trains led the new tourism economy to the great benefit of the town - the passengers alighting at ' Most Beautiful Bude, the Gem of the West.'

It was to this 'Gem of the West' that first my mother in 1931 and then Dad in 1946 came to set up in business for the first time on their own account and to raise their family.

V

Wroes
13 Belle Vue

Belle Vue Bude April 1957. The main street of the town. The Cornwall constabulary with duckling in one hand and white gloves in the other on escort duty giving safe passage to important members of the Bude community en route to the nearby river Neet. The new Wroes shop with tapered awnings opposite the single parked car in its second year of trading in Belle Vue.

Photo the Adrian Abbott collection.

It is 1956 and the Ball family is on the move. We are going up in the world in every sense. We are moving from The Strand to Belle Vue, number 13 to be precise, and to Mum and Dad's new acquisition the haberdashers' and outfitters' store Dinnis Medland. Mum and Dad have acquired the freehold which includes first floor accommodation, comprising best front room, sitting room, three bedrooms, two doubles and a single, and kitchen dining area with access directly onto a flat roof area overlooking Summerleaze Beach and the breakwater. And, what's more, the WC is separate to the bathroom. A quantum leap forward for convenience and a diminishing of breakfast hour arguments that have attached to morning ablution queues. The family still retains 18 The Strand.

Okay, so we've moved from living over one shop, to living over another, but we now pay rates and have become home owners. Belle Vue has us also moving up in the world geographically. We are half way up the hill that leads to Bude Picture House at the top of the town. We can say goodbye to the hazards of flooding along The Strand.

Belle Vue has a front door and a back door, also approached from a high sided dark alley directly off the pavement. Our front door is at 90 deg to Belle Vue and behind the eastern end shop window. Up half a landing, and the door in front of you gives access to the shop with the stairs turning through 180 deg and then a further 180 deg before arriving at our new home. Brown lino has given way to a richly patterned red stair carpet.

Adjacent to the small door from the shop onto the stairs is a shelf. On this shelf Dad places a World War Two field telephone in a rectangular timber box with a winding handle on the side. At the top of the stairs and the start of our home George Cornish comes in to fit a new worktop next to the south facing window upon which is to be located our telephone to the outside world. Our number is Bude 264, and another receiver is hard wired down to the field telephone with its distinct whirring noise from when the handle is cranked in the shop below.

Whilst Wroes of Bude business protocols might not quite match those of Ernie Yeo and Mrs Yeo at Cook's Stores in the Strand, there are strict observances required to give Mum and Dad and the whole family a degree of domestic privacy. None of the shop staff is allowed beyond this door. If any customer asks for Mum and Dad and they are above, the field telephone rings to summon a family member.

Mum and Dad's bedroom, the largest of the three, is on the south side with their bay window looking out across Summerleaze and the Breakwater. I share a room with brother Chris and our window looks onto Belle Vue. Falling asleep and waking up here is very different to The Strand. Cars change gear half way up Belle Vue. Each late evening Bude police mount a foot patrol round the town. They wear black constabulary capes with chrome chain neck fixings catching the street light. They check the shop keepers have properly locked up for the night and the rattle of door handles is an association of lullabies.

Life in Belle Vue soon settles down. With both Chris and Jenny away at boarding school, and Chris soon to depart to London University on a Cornwall County scholarship he has secured, I am left to my own devices. Paddy Frost and I spend hours in the loft with our Hornby 00 train set laid out on a permanent basis and expanded with each Christmas and birthday. We occasionally get into trouble but only of the most gentle kind. Aunty Win has given me a hurdy-gurdy for Christmas and Paddy and I do the rounds of the town securing pennies to augment our pocket money. I cannot recall Dad more furious than when he finds out and around the town we go once more returning all the pennies to our benefactors who had probably only donated in the first place in order to stop the hurdy-gurdy in its tracks.

My community is rich in opportunity for the enjoyment of the outdoors, our pastimes innocent and our pleasures simple. A favourite for Paddy and me is to visit the egg packing station on the upper wharf of Bude Canal in the days before it became Bude Band Room. A fierce looking engine drives pulleys and belts that connect to and shake large trays onto which the eggs are placed and graded to size. We are allowed to watch. We must stand well clear of the machinery. We stand next to a man in brown overalls who has a special job. With ink pad in one hand and rubber stamp in the other he carefully stamps little red lions on the eggs that achieve the top standard. The eggs are then packed and ready for despatch.

But the egg packing machinery is of naught compared to the fascination of being alongside retained fireman Bill Pickard. Bill is our friend. He lives in nearby Marhamchurch and each day pushbikes down the canal tow-path to Bude to discharge his town duties. Discharge is the word in every sense. Up on the cliffs at Compass Point and close by what we all call the Pepper Pot, the old watch tower, is a manhole cover with a big padlock. Bill is the holder of the keys to this padlock.

Often we hover about, just after the top of the tide knowing this is when Bill will arrive, puffing his way over the Downs up to this high cliff side point. We can join him in his work. Beneath the manhole cover is a set of concrete steps. They lead all the way down through what is approaching the tallest cliffs hereabouts to what is known to all as 'sewer beach'. Here is a long sewerage outfall cast iron pipe of large circumference and cased in concrete. At the bottom of the cliffs Cornish miners have hewn out a vast chamber which is the holding tank for all Bude's sewage.

The long sea outfall, Sewer Beach at the base of Compass Point. The tunnel gives access to the sewerage chamber and steps up through the cliffs.

Photo The Adrian Abbott Collection

At the bottom of the steps there is an enormous winding handle on a circular steel plate set into the side of the chamber. Bill allows us to watch whilst he hand operates the mechanism that opens the sluice that despatches the accumulation of Bude's human effluent to go out to sea with the ebb tide. We are not the only spectators to this. It attracts the entirety of the local seagull population and is feasting time for the scavenger fish, mackerel. These in turn are landed to feed the local population and complete the cycle.

Dad has finally succumbed to the persuasion that us having a television is long over due, but only after one of those events, the memory of which never fades. Mr Bartrop's wireless and television shop is now directly opposite us and he is chums with Dad as a fellow businessman in the town. Mr Bartrop was later to drown along with the local photographer Frank Dempster while attempting to round Barrel Rock returning from a fishing trip and being overwhelmed by a savage following sea.

The lengths to which Mr Bartrop has gone to convince Dad that our gathering around the wireless days are past involves the Ball family spending an evening, after all the shops have closed, sitting in Bartrop's shop window in the town watching television with the good people of Bude in turn watching us.

Never mind London, it is very rare indeed that we get experience of life beyond Cornwall. Of course, we know no different and we are certainly not deprived with Bude Sea Pool, surf beaches and cliff walks and the rolling Cornish countryside we have, for each month of the year, that which our summer visitors come to enjoy for just a few weeks. Annual family holidays are what other people do, not us. It is an 'inward to Bude, not an outward from Bude' concept.

Mum and Dad are united in the loving, untroubled way our home lives are run. That is so long as we stick closely to Dad's rules. Never do we have an electric light on after dark in a room except if we are there and it is necessary. 'We do not own shares in the 'lectric company' is Dad's regular scolding each time we forget. The concept of work ethic is instilled in us from an early age. This starts with the beginning of the day ... 'lying in bed all day will not buy the baby new shoes ...'

It was to pass that I never was to draw a day's dole in all my working life. I didn't dare. Dad would have been horrified. 'Get off your backside and get a job - any job, hard work is the rent we pay for life.'

Dad's view of life has been forged by the ignominy of the failure of the Ball family bakery business in Launceston midway through the First World War in 1916, severing his education at 14 years of age. The family leaving the Westgate Street home with Dad pushing all remaining family possessions on a hand cart was an indelible moment that never left him. These unwelcomed circumstances found him the same year in a London of the horse drawn Hansom cab, a World War being run by Prime Minister Asquith and accommodation in a modest garret over his employer's emporium - here at such a tender age, alone, owned by an employer who would not even allow him time off to attend his own father's funeral. Here was an early life founded on deprivation, self reliance and hardship. This frugality fed the pensive recollections that were shared with us and informed our own early lives. The switching off of the lights, the saving of cupfuls of petrol, all arise from Dad's hardship-haunted early years. Alongside all this is the often expressed parental advice that our best friend through life will be the pound in our pocket. Our values, our education and our inspiration are his lifetime's focus; his barometer to a brighter future than existed in Cornwall at the turn of the 20th Century.

Mum has never had to compete with Corky for motherly love but securing the right balance of my allegiance between Belle Vue and Kings Hill is clearly something that constantly occupies the front of her mind. When I am nine and can walk home from school alone she makes a point of leaving the shop floor each afternoon to ensure she is there to greet my homecoming. I must not dally or she will be worried and a new daily ritual is established. As I mount the stairs I shout 'Muthurr - I'm home' only to receive my daily scolding for improper pronunciation. Mum

places great emphasis on the sense of right and wrong, always telling the truth and the concepts of decency and social justice, doing the right thing. It is Mum who insists one particular Christmas Day morning that we slog off to another part of Bude to visit a family she knows to be on hard times, insisting we make sacrifices to their

Duckpool c1950. A Ball family favourite for picnics and birthday treats.
Photo Ball family archive.

needs. I give up one of my Christmas presents for their son of similar age to me.

For my birthday treat in June Mum takes some pals and me to Duckpool, a secluded beach a few miles north of Bude where we have great fun with ploppers - throwing beach pebbles into the water and damming the stream at the head of the beach where it flows to the Atlantic. We all sit down for our picnic birthday tea and we come to the birthday cake that Mum has bought, not having had time from her busy business day to make me one. We slice the cake and it is mouldy. I look into Mum's eyes with upset and despair only to see mirrored in her eyes a greater upset. The moment passes but never fades and in turn, and in time, becomes my own pensive recollection that speaks so much of these times.

Each year after Christmas time, soon into the New Year, we have the most unusual morning wake-up call of all. It is then that Wroes has its annual sale. Mum and Dad are frantically engaged from the day after our Boxing Day outing to Trevone ticketing the eagerly awaited bargains. On the first day of the sale I awake early to a hubbub outside and below my bedroom window as the crack of dawn sale queue forms. Dad always puts on his smartest suit for opening the shop on this special morning. With a turn of the key he sweeps the door back with a broad proprietorial smile says 'Good morning ladies' only to be swept aside in their rush to the bargains.

Neither Mum nor Dad has time or inclination for much of a social life beyond running the shop. In 1950 Dad has become a founder member of the Rotary Club of Bude and both Mum and Dad support and are involved in the local Chamber of Trade. It is only for Rotary President's Night and the Chamber of Trade Christmas dinner that we see Mum and Dad in their finery and out on the town. This sets the social benchmark for our household and places our parents in no difficulty with the management of our own expectations.

What is clear is that Mum and Dad are a great team. They have complementary skills and a dedication to developing their business: a true fifty-fifty partnership but one that does not come without personal sacrifice. For Dad his presence on the shop floor to meet and greet each customer is a given. His interpersonal skills are exemplary; his natural charm endless and there is never a hair out of place, nor a word wanting. He has an excellent eye for colour and design. His later London years

The founding members of the Rotary Club of Bude 1950.

Back row (left to right) Bryan T.W.Bartlett, L Rich,Reg Bartop, Jim E Westwood, Chris E Ball, Derek H Ridler, Frank Ring-Santler, K Laurie N Barnett, Raymond Pethick, R.C Walters.
Front row (left to right) Spencer Thorn, Bill Parsons, Jim Veale, Walter Prest, C Harry Walter, C Victor French, E Metherell Gard, O.L Cory, W Marsh
      Dad back row, fifth from left next to Derek Ridler on his left. Together they stood surety for Teddy Hemmerle to remain in Bude at the end of the war. Centre front President Harry Walter who secured Bude SLSC its name, and to his right Rev Walter Prest who was responsible for our pastoral care at Bude Primary School.

Photo The Rotary Club of Bude.

working in the famous Heals department store and then Dingles of Plymouth have honed his skills. He is consummate in attention to detail in layout of shop floor, window dressing and fulfilling every expectation of a discerning customer.

To this partnership Mum brings unrivalled book keeping skills. Her years of keeping the books at Bude Steam Laundry and the United Hunts' Club in London's Mayfair sit alongside a newly acquired talent for ladies

Bude sea pool c1955 where all of us learned to swim.

Photo Adrian Abbott collection.

corsetry and undergarments. She knows her customers, she understands their needs. Her customers know they can rely on her implicitly. This bond of trust establishes a loyal and profitable clientele. But it is only profitable because Mum knows exactly, to the penny, where the money goes. All through her life she remains exceptionally numerate. It is a strength that never leaves her.

Living by the sea places high emphasis on learning to swim at an early age and from as soon as we can remember we are all taught to swim in Bude Sea Pool, or Tommy's Pit, at the end of the Breakwater. The goal for us all is 25 yards for which we all receive a certificate. Each one of us in the class is incentivised to achieve this milestone in our lives growing up in Bude.

Dad has a very precise routine in the mornings timed to within a few minutes for shop opening hours and start of the day's business. He is not best pleased to be dragged down early one morning to Bude Sea Pool in order to watch me swim my 25 yards, the prerequisite witnessing before a special pocket money pay out. There stands Dad in his smart suit, impatient, puffing away on his Woodbine as I swim towards him to claim my reward and praise.

In truth drownings are a regular feature on Cornish beaches at this

Press release

COMMONWEALTH OF AUSTRALIA

News and Information Bureau,

Australia House, Strand, W.C.2.

TEMple Bar 2435

28th July, 1953.

AUSTRALIAN HELPS FORMATION OF SURF
LIFE-SAVING CLUB IN CORNWALL

   Britain's first surf live-saving club, organised wholly on Australian surf life-saving principles, will be formed at Bude, Cornwall, next week.

   Formation of the club is being arranged by Mr. Allan Kennedy, a well-known Australian surf life-saver who is a former superintendent of surf life-saving for Queensland and Victoria, a life member of the Surf Life-Saving Association of Australia and the Association's representative in Britain.

   The Australian High Commissioner, Sir Thomas White, himself a keen surfer and a former President of the Royal Life-Saving Society, is taking close interest in the introduction to Britain of Australian surf life-saving principles.

   Next week-end at Bude, Mr. Kennedy begins the training of prospective members of the Bude Club. For a week he will instruct local swimmers in general surf life-saving routines, including reel and belt work, resuscitation methods, rescues and releases and the handling of the surf ski.

   The Australian Surf Life-Saving Association has sent to Britain a fully-equipped reel, line and belt and an Australian surf ski measuring 14 ft. 3 ins. by 2 ft. 3 ins. Demonstrations in the use of the ski will be given at Bude by Mr. Kennedy next week-end and throughout the following week.

   An Australian invention, the surf ski is widely used for rescue work on Australian ocean beaches. It is a cross between the flat surf board and the canoe and is the fastest craft for getting from beach through surf to a bather in difficulties. The ski is propelled by a double-ended paddle and is large enough to carry a "patient" in addition to the surf life-saver.

. . . .

The Commonwealth of Australia Press Release July 1953 at the founding of Bude Surf Life Saving Club (SLSC).

     Image courtesy of Ron Rankin AM, President Surf Life Saving Australia.

        Archive Surf Life Saving Australia

BBC outside broadcast 1954 covering the establishment of surf life saving in Great Britain, Crooklets Beach Bude.

Photo courtesy Ron Rankin AM President Surf Life Saving Australia
Archive Surf Life Saving Australia

time, so regular in fact that such an occurrence only secures a small paragraph on the inside pages of the Western Morning News. To meet this shameful circumstance in 1953 The Bude Surf Life Saving Club is formed by an Australian Allan Kennedy, who declares Bude to be Britain's 'Bondi'. We are the first Surf Life Saving Club to be formed in Great Britain. It is based on Australian surf life saving techniques and the club soon becomes a leading youth organisation in our community. Several public meetings are held and support for this worthy endeavour moves forward at a pace.

The main concern surrounds what our new club is to be called. The local hoteliers are united against the club being called the Bude Surf Life Saving Club. In their eyes it implies that Bude is a dangerous place to spend your holidays and you are at risk of drowning on our beaches. A further public meeting is called in order for them to express their anxieties. These are only finally set aside by the intervention of Harry

Gun battery ATS training at Cleave Camp. The huts where Teddy and I go on Saturdays on Woolacotts business.   *Photo Bill Young (decd)/the Adrian Abbott collection*

Walter, another of Dad's chums and fellow founder Rotarian in the town. Rising to his feet he reminded those in attendance at the charged meeting that for many years now Bude had enjoyed the services of the Bude Fire Brigade. This did not, however, mean that Bude had been constantly on fire. The day was won.

My early swimming proficiency has come from the endless hours on Summerleaze Beach and being taught by Teddy and Jean. Sister Jenny also develops her swimming skills in this way as do countless youngsters with Jean and Teddy's enthusiasm for this task eventually bringing the Junior Surf Life Saving Club Nippers organisation into being.

Most Saturdays, which is a work day for Teddy, sees me joining him in Woolacotts van with regular visits to Cleave Camp just beyond Duckpool to the north of Bude. Cleave is an Army anti-aircraft gun battery training establishment with one of its most notable wartime personnel being Mary Soames, daughter of Winston Churchill. Mary, who served in the ATS, departed Bude to be an ADC to her father when Prime Minister.

Our regular Saturday morning visits to Cleave Camp are for a special reason. There is a personnel changeover every two or three weeks with troops arriving and departing Bude Railway Station. Each changeover sees us attending the Sergeant's Mess for handover and settlement of toasters and wirelesses on hire from Woolacotts, Teddy's employer.

During the working week Teddy is in great demand for installing televisions. Despite fierce opposition from Prime Minister Churchill, Parliament narrowly determines that cameras should be allowed inside Westminster Abbey to televise the Coronation. There is quite a flourish of demand to have a set installed in time to view this grand State occasion and Teddy is kept very busy.

George Lyle, the rabbit man, described by Teddy as Lord Mayor of Stratton, has been a kindly benefactor to Teddy since his prisoner of war days. He gets priority service to have an installation in time for the big event. The television signal to Bude is first beamed over in 1952 from the mast at Wenvoe just outside Cardiff. By the time it has crossed the Bristol Channel and come in around Barrel Rock it is tired, foggy and resembles a snow storm. Teddy signs off his successful installation with George Lyle and together they look at the flickering screen. 'ere Teddy.' says George, 'us 'ave got better weather in Cornwall than they got up in London.'

The Coronation apart I recall little of other affairs of State or beyond that enters our radar as primary school children. The one possible exception is the Suez Crisis of 1956 and only then because Dad is thought to be the spitting image of Prime Minister Anthony Eden and this creates a connection that regularly crops up in conversation. Dad

Ball family photograph Marina, Kings Hill front lawn 1956 with dad aka Prime Minister Anthony Eden.

Photo Ball family Archive.

has been waiting for the Atlantic Coast Express at Waterloo. He has requested a cup of tea from the station buffet and is just about to take his refreshment from the tea lady when she is rebuked by her colleague – 'You can't give the Prime Minister tea in a cracked cup.' I think my only concern on hearing that our country might again be in conflict is anxiety about the return of ration books for sweets and chocolate, which has only recently been abandoned.

Often we receive visits from travelling salesmen and a few of these regular faces have become chums with Mum and Dad. There are some wonderful vehicles purpose designed for the travelling salesman who are all referred to as 'Travellers'. They park up in Belle Vue directly opposite the shop in specially designed vans of curious shape with a single door at the back allowing Mum and Dad to enter and inspect garments that have travelled to Bude on rails.

Mum has a special eye tuned to her customers and word will be conveyed via Bude 264 that a new range of garments can now be viewed or 'taken on appro'. That is taken home for approval and endorsement by the head of household, or returned if not quite suitable or not within the family budget this month.

Not long after we arrive in Belle Vue Jean and Teddy are also on the move. On 5th November, bonfire night, they leave the Duchy Bakeries flat and move to 44 Lynstone Road on the way out to Widemouth Bay. This house is owned by Mr Parkhouse, Bude's main building contractor and George and Micky's employer. They secure the tenancy at a cost of five shillings a week. This is on the basis that Teddy will do Parkhouse's garden, as he lives opposite overlooking the canal.

However this gardening arrangement only starts with the arrival of next spring. Teddy obtains consent to redecorate his new house. On arrival it is painted top to bottom in brown, green and cream paint. Curiously Cleave Camp is painted in the same colours, the paint being identical to War Office issue. He is able to do the redecorating over the winter as he is not required on gardening duty. Sadly Mr Parkhouse dies before the spring. Jean and Teddy thus become sitting tenants. They don't remain sitting tenants at 'five bob' a week for very long because this circumstance allows them to purchase the house at a very advantageous price.

I have moved to Miss Maddock's class on the north west side of the school nestling underneath the west Shalder Hill sand dune. Home

Bude CSSM at Crooklets Beach, c1956.
Photo Anna McDougall / Nostalgic Bude

life is not bookish in any way. I have not been deprived of bedtime stories but there is no reverence attached to reading or to books in the Ball family life. This is why an inscribed Bible received at Easter is of such import. Inside the front cover it says 'To Jonathan with love from Daddy and Mummy Easter 1956.' And there is a riveting whole page frontispiece colour painting of Samson killing a young lion with his bare hands 'And he rent him as he would have a kid'. Judges 14.5. This image is the most thumbed page of any book I am to receive at this time, albeit there are two more books that come my way in special circumstances.

My new teacher Miss Maddock lives with her Mum, but it is thought she has private family money. She drives around in a racy open topped sports car which is slightly incongruous for a dedicated spinster lady who is so evidently conservative and Christian in her every thought word and deed. She is held in special regard and fondness for a certain reason: each child who goes through her class receives, at her expense, a small New Testament Bible, personally inscribed as a keepsake of the year in our lives we share with her.

And there is one more book that makes 1956 so special. It comes from the CSSM, the Children's Special Service Mission. Each summer they come to the town to promote Christian teachings and traditions and this is a central focus of several weeks of our summer holidays on Bude beach. We have great fun, outside all day with lots of organised activities. These are substantially run by university student volunteers, with strong Christian credentials under the superintendence of the saintly Quintin Carr who wears long khaki shorts and a brightly striped university rowing blazer. His organisational skills are founded on fun and inspiration.

Each day starts with us building an enormous sand pulpit at the back of Crooklets Beach and the girls decorate the pulpit front with limpet shells, pebbles and wild flowers. We erect the CSSM banner and help manhandle the ancient harmonium into its position alongside the newly constructed pulpit. We start with prayers and then proceed with an evangelical fervour standing up for our favourite hymns sung with wild arm actions ...

'Wide, wide as the ocean...
High as the heavens above,
Deep, deep as the deepest sea
Is my Saviour's Love.
I, though so unworthy, still am a child of his care,
For his word teaches me, that his love reaches me,
Everywhere'

with a vast sweep of our arms and great emphasis on the last word.

Then we all sit down and we think about this. Quintin Carr gently gives us lessons for life and gentle slants on Biblical stories. Then it's off to fight the tide - who can build the largest sand castle that lasts the longest against the incoming waves - and sausage sizzles at Earthquake Beach where we sit around a camp fire, sing songs and have more Bible stories. No one thinks this is sissy and the foundation stones of our

CSSM Prize 1956
Ball family Archive

91

Christian ideals are erected in these weeks of summer beach fun.

Every year the CSSM has an annual sand modelling competition. This year I win first prize. As far as I can remember I have never won a prize for anything and therefore to stand up in front of all my chums and walk forward and receive a Scripture Union book prize is a very memorable moment indeed. The book is 'Eyes on Jungle Doctor' and is taken home and devoured. It's all about an Australian Missionary from Adelaide and his life in Tanganyika. The dust jacket describes it as being 'profusely illustrated' and so it is. It is full of far away images of black men holding spears and 'Bwana' on every page - sounds and sights of Empire serving the missionary cause. I have to look at the map on the classroom wall to check how far away Adelaide and Tanganyika are from Cornwall.

Dr Anthony Blood, 1958, the year he featured as a country GP in the BBC television series Your Life in Their Hands. Shown here wearing his customary Homburg hat. For 35 years he had special responsibility for obstetrics within the Practice area in rural north Cornwall and always wore a flower in his buttonhole when conducting ante natal clinics.

Photo Ball/Blood family archive

With Chris at the London School of Economics and Jenny at boarding school in Bournemouth my primary education is soon to conclude in the innocence in which it began, the post war bulge class of 46 pupils with little comings and goings for the greater part of what, to us, has been a changeless decade.

In 1958 there is an expectation of us that hitherto had passed us by. We are coming up to what we are told is the Eleven Plus examination and Mr Luke's emphasis on discipline now sits alongside endeavour. We are now in Mr Jury's class and his nickname is 'Pop Jury'. His wife Mrs Jury is a

Winter wind-blown snowdrifts, 1962.

Photo the Adrian Abbott collection

Sister at Stratton Cottage Hospital which has propelled sleepy Bude into the national limelight.

In February of this year a popular television documentary programme called 'Your Life in Their Hands' selects our local General Practitioner, Dr Blood, as the representative of the nation's GPs, to explain the more eccentric workings of the newly fledged National Health Service. TV is now a part of all our lives. We all sit glued to our black and white television screens watching Dr Blood on his medical rounds being chased by the Cornwall Ambulance Service with bells ringing to recover a farm worker from the middle of nowhere. The horizontal patient is examined by Dr Blood, with the snow falling and the good doctor puffing away on his pipe that does not leave his mouth. It is then back to Stratton Cottage Hospital with Dr Blood undertaking minor surgery in front of the BBC outside broadcast cameras. We are told this is the first time surgery has been shown live on British television.

There on the front lawns of the hospital is a charming summer house. It has a small front veranda all mounted on a turntable. Periodically during the afternoons the nurses come out to swing the summer house round to follow the afternoon sun on this convalescence carousel.

Little, if any, patient confidentiality concerns the BBC or Dr Harold Holtby, Bude's senior practitioner in charge of the programme. He

93

conveys the clear impression that this Cottage Hospital is a vital and much respected institution within our remote rural community. As the TV cameras move around the wards deference combines with cheery expressions of wanting the world to know that we, the people of Bude and Stratton, are very proud of our medical facilities whilst the opportunity to point out shortcomings is not missed.

A farmer's wife highlights a particular new health service bureaucratic nonsense besetting the time. Looking straight at the camera she declares 'if we was to be able to have our babies 'ere in Stratton, t'wd be a perfect boon.'

The programme concludes with the last word given to young Dr Anthony Blood sat in Matron's sitting room in Stratton Cottage Hospital, in front of the fire and drinking a glass of her sherry. Having been challenged about choosing to be a GP in such a rural area, his reply is that for him, being a GP is not a career it is a way of life. He makes the point that the nearest General Hospital at Plymouth is two and a half hours away by ambulance. The new breed of National Health General Practitioners serving the rural outposts, such as where we live, have to make their life and death decisions unaided and three hours before the vast majority of medical practitioners and consultants based in better populated areas. Little did I know that sixteen years later he was to become my father-in-law.

And so my time at Bude Primary School comes to its conclusion a few months later in the summer of 1958. I have passed the 11+ examination and I am to follow in my brother Chris's footsteps to board at Truro School. Mum and Dad place the highest possible value on our education. Any and all spare cash that might otherwise go on holidays, home improvements, new cars or suchlike is reserved exclusively for our education. Both Truro School and Talbot Heath, Bournemouth, are Direct Grant schools. It is this that just makes them within Mum and Dad's ability to pay the fees.

A tree-lined snaking drive steeply inclined past grassy terraces each containing a tennis court, heightens the sense of arrival at the imposing front elevation of Truro School which, for us boarders who outnumber day boys, is a true bastion of Cornish Methodism. We are inducted into a rigid regime of starched collars and studs, chapel twice on Sunday and about eight hours a week of choir practice in the full Methodist tradition which is to force feed into me a life long love of singing.

Gathering for morning assembly on my first day in Truro School Chapel is a world away from Hedley Luke calling the register in the Shalder Hills sand dunes. It is all a question of scale. The school choir comfortably takes up at least six oak pews and competes with the school organ in belting out Sagina, Blaenwern, Cwm Rhondda and other rousing hymn tunes from the Methodist hymn book. John Wesley's heroic journeying has not been in vain.

Anyone navigating Bude's history and geography soon realises it is the sea which most shapes the culture, values and strong sense of belonging of its inhabitants. For all of my growing up years thus far I have lived no more than yards from this wild, rugged windswept coastline of North Cornwall. And so, for the first time the rhythm of my daily life no longer attaches to tide and shoreline. It is now governed by the clang of the enormous hand rung school bell hanging outside the window on the first stair landing of the main school front building. There is a rosta in Senior School for bell ringing duty. It is this mighty school bell that controls all our waking moments. With the tolling of this bell I am leaving my childhood behind. I am also saying goodbye to the west Shalder Hill sand dune soon to disappear in a monumental act of civic vandalism. For the academic year at least it is cheerio to being close by the seagulls' cry.

VI

Boarding School
1958-1965

The main front elevation of Truro School under floodlights from the snaking front drive.
Photo Truro School

'High on the Hill with the city below up in the sunshine we live' is our appalling school song. It is I suppose geographically accurate but is otherwise in sharp conflict with the dignified sense of purpose conveyed in the school prospectus. The school motto, esse quam videri, to be rather than to see, is our watchword.

Truro School had been established in 1880, by which time Methodism in Cornwall had triumphed as it did particularly in Wales and other mining communities. John Wesley's preachings mined a rich seam. For many Cornish folk the Church of England did not serve them well, for others he was an unwelcomed new voice. It is recorded that a school boy chant of the time was 'Mr Wesley's come to town, to try to pull our churches down'. Methodism was born in song and Thomas Merritt, miner's son and organist at Illogan Methodist Chapel, held great sway and influence as a prolific writer of Cornish carols.

Meanwhile Cornwall's Celtic saints maintained their hold undiminished. Parallel with the Methodist Foundation establishing Truro School came the movement that was to build a Cathedral with Edward Benson appointed the first Bishop of Truro. It was Benson who conceived the service of Nine Lessons and Carols so loved and adopted by the Anglican community world wide. But it was to Thomas Merritt that the Cornish miner in Moonta, South Australia, and Grass Valley California turned at Christmas time.

In the history of Truro School written by archivist Joanna Wood is a greater insight into these Victorian times. Whether Truro School was indeed founded as a counter balance to the newly emerging Diocese of Truro with the building of Truro Cathedral, we will never know. What, however, is not in question is that the school's aim was to provide boys with an education based on ' a foundation of truth, the principle of all

Christian morality, which it was thought alone can make a worthy British citizen.'

Seventy eight years later there seems no hurry in parting company with these ideals and values. Jesus Christ enters our lives every day, usually more than once. He comes with a broad Cornish accent from passionate Local Circuit preachers. He comes with the impeccable Queen's English and fine oratory of headmaster and School Chaplain.

He comes in Latin with the sung school Grace:

Benedic, Domine, nobis et scholae nostrae
 quam ad Majorem Tuam Gloriam curamus
constituendam per Jesum Christum Dominum Nostrum

and also at our mealtimes in the dining hall, standing to attention whilst the Head Boy proclaims

Bendictus Benedicat per Jesum Christum Dominum Nostrum

The enormous school dining hall accommodates row upon row of huge oak refectory tables, is oak panelled and with a raised dais at the west end for Masters' dining; altogether a grandeur sadly not matched by the fare. I soon learn I am not the only new boy to have a problem with scale.

In my first term I do not recall being homesick. My first year boarding house is Poltisco, a large Regency building on Malpas Road which sleeps about 20 of us. Nearby are three teaching huts and between us and Malpas Road is the Scout Hut. A long steep footpath climbs to the school chapel and Main School where all boarders dine together. We are allowed into Truro for an hour and a half on Wednesday afternoons and in my first year I spend some of this precious time each week being fed by Aunt Edie in the family owned shop W W Edwards at the bottom of Lemon Street.

The City of Truro is dominated by John Loughborough Pearson's Cathedral. Early morning mists often hug the valley leaving just the Cathedral spires in our view where this imposing building meets the sky above. Below us from our bird's eye view we have a pattern book of Cornish history. There are granite sets to pavements, roads and squares, open leets for charm and Iron Dukes for comfort stops where we pee through a trough directly into the rivers Kenwyn and Allen running below. The streetscapes predating the City status conferred by the Cathedral and ordained and declared by Queen Victoria in 1877 have not yet been swept away. The Cornish hewn paving stones serve the interests of the pedestrian before those of the motorist.

I have joined the 3rd Truro (Truro School) Scout Troop as an opportunity for escape from the strictly enforced school bounds with the added attraction of annual Scout Camps in Wales and Scotland. In charge is the geography and geology Master, Leonard J Penna, a wiry, eccentric bachelor Cornishman, whiskery yet without a beard, with a whiny voice and fussy, fastidious temperament which earns him the nickname 'Faff'. Whether it is our shared sense of Cornish belonging I am not sure, but over the years he becomes my 'Mr Chips' and remains a strong influence throughout my school years. I am richly rewarded by having a guiding star to chart my progress through the school with his school report comments, in an elegant hand and often with turquoise ink

The Third Truro (Truro School) Scout Troop in grounds of Pentreve boarding house. Scout Master Leonard Penna, in white shorts seated immediately behind scout in dark blazer. I am top row, 4th from right.

Photo Truro School / Ball family archive

101

from a Parker fountain pen, the most generous I receive.

We depart Truro Railway Station by steam train bound for scout camp in Scotland under Mr Penna's eccentric leadership. In my patrol is a farmer's son who has never been on a train or north of Truro in his life. At Paddington Station we spill out onto the platform whereupon he 'literally' freezes, gazing upwards in awe and wonder at the heroic Isambard Kingdom Brunel's cavernous structure and memorably utters – 'My gar – you couldn't 'alf store some 'ay in 'ere'.

Mr Penna selects a small group of young scouts for what he terms a weekend endurance hike across the moors of West Penwith beginning at Penzance railway station. We arrive in the spring of 1959 to start what is a truly magical journey across the granite uplands of the Land's End peninsula. We are in the Penwith Hundred, the most westerly of Cornwall's ancient Hundreds with my own Stratton Hundred, the most northerly, embracing the Bude area up to the border of Devonshire – more usually referred to as England. I am about to get my first subliminal lesson in connecting geology, landscape and archaeology. If I am to look back on one weekend in my formative years that was to forge my future most powerfully, surely this is it.

Rising out of Penzance are the Merry Maidens, the first of the Cornish antiquities. These Bronze Age beauties are a stone circle of pillars of granite to which attach various theories – astronomical and religious – but as Mr Penna explains, the Cornish will always go with the yarn that these maidens were turned into stone for their merry dancing on the Sabbath.

Over the weekend he introduces us to Boscawen-Un, Chysauster, a classic courtyard Bronze Age village, Chun Castle, ancient Hill fort with Chun Quoit close by, the holed stone at Men-an-tol where we ceremoniously pass our bodies through. This we are told is an ancient Cornish cure for rickets. And then the Fogou at Pendeen Vau. Fogou – what a lovely word - derives from the Cornish for cave. Chysauster, Carn Euny, Boscawen-Un, on they go, all bedrock of our Cornish heritage and our Cornish language. How fitting that Pendeen Vau is close to Pendeen House the family home of Dr William Borlase who was born there in 1696. Mr Penna tells us he wrote The Antiquities of Cornwall in 1758, the Bible on these matters. So important is he that we have the Borlase Society at Truro School which delivers our lessons in archaeology. His name is synonymous with these treasured stones which owe their vandal-free survival to their geological hardness and Cornish respect handed down through the centuries.

Our master in charge has a passion for all these sights which is infectious. I am not sure whether it was on this trip or in later years during A level geology lessons that he extols to us the immutability of granite even to weathering in this most wild of landscapes explaining that course grained granite will last for ever and fine grained granite a day longer. Isn't that what a good teacher is all about?

If you seek further insight into these granite uplands read the poetry and prose of Arthur Caddick, the post war Penwith poet who, for 35 years, lived here in a remote cottage aptly named 'Windswept' near Nancledra. Sometimes referred to as the Dylan Thomas of Cornwall and with every justification given Arthur displayed a similar fondness for the pint which probably hindered his wider recognition. There is no finer aid to a better understanding of the magic that is West Penwith than his intoxicating poetry and prose which captures the connection between Cornish landscape and identity. He is buried in Ludgvan Churchyard and quite possibly buried with him is his favourite walking stick upon which he had inscribed what could serve as his most fitting epitaph:

'Good Bacchus, guard these steps of mine
And keep me safe from sin
And, if I stumble, let me fall
Outside a decent inn.'

I guess it might have been these proclivities that excludes this contemporary Cornish poet from entering the curriculum at Truro School. My English teacher Ken W D James is a Welshman and fanatical about rugby and cricket. I think it's fair to say that rugby, singing and academe all sit side by side in significance and emphasis. We still bask in the glory of old boy John Kendall-Carpenter whose war years at Truro School were followed by gaining three rugby blues at Oxford before going on to captain England to great acclaim. In addition to playing for the Barbarians and his home club Penzance-Newlyn he had many caps for the Cornwall county team. Here in Cornwall the county rugby team is followed with religious fervour. Whenever Cornwall plays at home, the school lays on a bus for us to go and watch. Our hero is Richard Sharp who captains Cornwall and England. If not God, he's certainly one of the disciples. As Captain of England in 1963 playing in the Calcutta Cup against Scotland he scores the most inspirational try any of us have ever seen.

Rugby and singing at Truro School have a special link for me. I join the school choir in my first term and by the time my voice is about to break I am the head of more than 20 trebles. With the altos, tenors and bases this is a formidable choir and we have a powerful presence. Our music master, Kenneth Pelmear is a Mr Rugby in Cornwall. He has written the seminal volume 'Rugby in the Duchy', the official history of the game in Cornwall. Not only this, but he has also penned the music to the Cornish anthem 'Hail to the Homeland' which sits immediately below Trelawny in the hearts of most Cornishmen. It is a favourite within the Cornish male voice choir tradition.

Kenneth Pelmear is one of the world's enthusiasts and is an inspiration to us all. To have him as our choir master is, for me, a joy. He is a male voice choir and brass band man first, but the length and breadth of his musical knowledge mean the school's reputation for music prospers. This is not solely confined to the expressions of Cornish culture. The school gives more than a nod to contemporary pop music with fellow pupil, drummer Roger Taylor fronting our lively popular music scene. When his legendary band Queen emerge onto the pop scene their first live performance takes place in Truro City Hall in 1970.

We are a large boarding community and are thrown into a wide range of activities. Whenever there is a General Election we hold our own version. Day boy David Penhaligon who in time becomes the distinguished sitting Member of Parliament for the Truro Constituency, secures his first political victory with us in the debating chamber of Truro School Chapel.

Every winter we have the dormitory play festival. Most of us are caught up one way or another in putting on plays. Several pupils go on to become household names as actors. There is also a poster competition to promote each House play which has its own dedicated art prize. This play festival dominates many long winter evenings. We are all incentivised to do well by our House as there is a tantalising prize. The winning dormitory celebrates with their exclusive party where they are served Cornish pasties and a bottle of Corona.

The festival takes place in the gymnasium, accommodated above the school Chapel and of the same substantial plan area. It is November

1963. We are mid way through the play festival. Our Biology Master Mr Shrimpton makes an unscheduled appearance in the middle of a performance. He walks to the front of the stage. The house lights go up. There is a stunned silence. We are told that John F Kennedy, President of the United States of America, has been shot and is dead.

The last evening of term before going home for Christmas has a role reversal with what is termed The Masters' Feast. Our modest fare gets a festive boost, served by our Masters who then entertain us with their own pantomime. This reinforces in our young lives the adage that the greatest mirth and enjoyment so often come from simple pleasures.

We are allowed exeats twice a term and these run from after Sunday morning service at St Mary's Methodist Church in Truro until 6pm evening chapel back at the school. Woe betide us if we are not back in good time. Our parents and guardians are encouraged to join us in school chapel. Mum and Dad always plead the long journey back to Bude in mitigation of their non attendance

Boarding school life takes on a different personality at weekends. Lessons run until Saturday lunch time after which sport and other extra curricular activities pass the time until Sunday evening chapel. We are excused Sunday morning service if we engage with these activities beyond the school bounds. These weekends define so many of the memories I take away from my boarding school years.

Scouting provides the opportunity for regular visits to the Atlantic coastline of Cornwall with groups of us in the charge of Mr Penna overnighting in youth hostels. Before the end of this decade we will have seen man walking on the moon. I have mused on many occasions about the fact that eleven out of the twelve men who have walked on the moon had been boy scouts in their youth. Scouting somehow defines my own life journey of exploration and discovery that so connects me with the coastal scenery of Cornwall. Mr Penna takes us around Cligga Head, Perranporth, explaining its incredible geology with tin and wolframite. In the same breath we have oceanography and ornithology pointed out; never to be forgotten lessons combining observation with respect.

On another occasion we find ourselves close by Holywell Bay where Mr Penna has a dwelling. It has been designed by Cornish architect and school old boy John Crowther. Mr Penna is the proud owner of a fine minerals collection. We are taken to his house. Between the hallway and the living room there is a plate glass wall with glass shelving to display

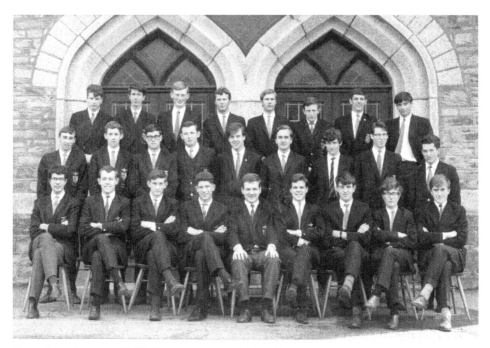

Truro School prefects 1965. I am top row, 2nd from right.

Photo Truro School / Ball family archive

the collection. The sunlight of the day glints upon Cornwall's crown jewels as connectivity is made between geology and architecture.

Perhaps the most lasting memory of this day is us all getting our feet wet. We are taken for a walk along the tide line. Suddenly we are stopped in our tracks by our leader. We look up and there majestically soaring in the thermals are a pair of Cornish Choughs. We are mesmerised and enthralled by the sight of these rare birds, emblems on the Cornwall coat of arms, exercising their ancestral freedom of the Duchy. None of us noticed the tide coming in.

I wish I could recount to you, dear reader, my many achievements during these years at Truro School but alas I can't. In academe and sporting prowess I am firmly middle order. Those kindly disposed would describe me as a late developer, a characteristic that survives well into my professional training. It is quite some years later in 1980 when I attend a reunion to mark the Centenary of the founding of Truro School and find myself face to face with Ken W D James. 'Ball isn't it? he enquires. 'Yes Sir' I reply. 'Tell me, what are you doing with yourself now?' 'I'm an Architect'. 'What - a real one?' 'Yes'. There is a long pause followed by 'Gooood Lord.' He turns away to other conversations and it is not long after this I hear of this Welshman's passing at which time I reflect that my enjoyment of rugby and the English language must have flowed from his teaching prowess.

Entering the Lower Sixth for my A level years finds me in the main school dormitory of Trennick, part of the original school buildings. Here the spartan and character forming ideals of our Wesleyan founders survive. It's long, narrow, high ceilinged with vertical sash windows on either side. The housemaster is Mr Penna. I am one of the two dormitory prefects. In winter months it's perishing. Mr Penna insists the windows are kept open to a minimum of six inches regardless of the outside temperature. He has two rooms of accommodation at the east end of the dormitory. His regular patrolling in the discharge of his housemaster duties become more of a prowl if he senses mischief afoot.

In the 6th form the choir continues to be a big part of my life. The most complex anthems and serious choral works can be mastered with ease. The bedrock of the school choral tradition has produced Benjamin Luxon, a distant cousin of mine, and Alan Opie, both acclaimed baritones. I am to sign off my school choir career with a performance of Bach's B Minor Mass in Truro Cathedral with John Shirley-Quirk, soloist.

The main area where I have added lustre to the school's reputation is with the chess team. I have followed my brother Chris who also served the chess team with distinction. I have represented the senior school team in competitive chess from about the age of 13. This includes winning my board when selected to play for the full Cornwall side which finds me presented with school colours and receiving the adulation of all in Morning Assembly the day following my notable victory. It is a special moment that I cherish.

Head of chess is my art master Cyril Smith. He also is an assistant scout master to the troop. We get on well. My chess team achievements cement our relationship, which in turn helps determine my future. It is his guidance that becomes so valuable as my thoughts turn to what I might be doing in the world.

With hindsight I much regret my lack of application both academically and particularly in rugby, which I have always greatly enjoyed. My rugby career was only to flourish upon leaving school for London and joining London Cornish RFC. Within a few weeks of joining the Club I am appointed Choirmaster, using the term in the loosest interpretation, to swing my arms around for the already enviable post-match singing reputation the Club enjoys.

My favourite A level subject is geology with regular field trips where we learn that Cornwall is the very best area of Great Britain for the study of geology and geomorphology. There are only two or three minerals traceable in Britain not present west of the River Tamar. The mnemonic layerings and dramatic stratifications of millennia with the sedimentary being metamorphosed by granite igneous extrusions have produced a landscape that has defined our social history.

The unseen hand of destiny may be at work as I tramp Kernick china clay pit. Here I learn all about the china clay industry and first understand the processes. China clay is not mined, dug or quarried. It is won. The winning of china clay is the term used for the extractive process, words that somehow defines the essence of the area. Thirty years later finds me in nearby Bodelva Pit. It is here we make the decision to site The Eden Project.

It is 1964 and Bob Dylan's song 'The times they are a-changing' is hated by Mr Penna but loved by the whole dormitory including the prefects. Already we have said goodbye to our Latin Grace in the dining hall. It is memorably replaced by Head Boy John Rhys-Davies during my fifth year. His rite of passage to acclaim by pupil and staff alike has come with his performance as Othello in the annual school play. The reviews reach the Cornwall press. With such imposing presence and his mellifluous Welsh voice our Grace is delivered in booming brevity, 'Thanks be to God, Amen carry on'. It is a dramatic delivery from someone

Jim Phelan tramp extraordinaire befriended by Dad with his forwarding address to stay in touch.   *Photo the Ball family archive.*

The Caps Ceremony for school leavers, Boscawen Bridge
Truro July 1965. I am 2nd from left.
Photo Truro School / Ball family archive

destined for theatrical stardom.

Let it not be said that the Ball family are not keeping up with these changing times. Over the seven years of boarding at Truro School Dad and I have got to know the road between Bude and Truro very well indeed. Dad's cars have gone from the Ford Pop to Consuls, to Zephyrs and then to a Mini when we become a two car family. Hitch-hiking is an accepted norm for youngsters and for tramps and journeymen who are regular in their appearance in the highways and byways of Cornwall in the years after the war. Dad has a sympathetic inclination to stop for hitch-hikers and tramps. As with so many things he has his own names for these gentlemen of the road. He refers to them as 'milestone inspectors'. On one occasion he picks up the master tramp of these times, a man by the name of Jim Phelan who has spent time in Dartmoor Prison. He detains Dad in a long conversation about the 'phoneys'.

Between St Columb Major and Ladock, in a copse beside the road, resides a favourite of Dad's who has chosen the wanderer's way of life. Dad has learnt the language of the road from Jim Phelan. Those tramps acknowledged as best of their breed are referred to as 'top-cocks'. The roads on which they journey are called 'the Toby'. Each time we pass this copse Dad toots the horn and we get a wave from its inhabitant sitting by his camp fire which never goes out. The smoke has stained his balding head as black as the embers in the fire.

My own hitch-hiking days are mainly in scout uniform and in the fifth form. By this time we have licence and freedom within the scout troop. With housemaster's permission we are able to take off on missions which we contrive and for which we have gained approval. This new found freedom allows even greater exploration of West Cornwall including, in November 1962, witnessing the wreck of the Jean Gougy, a French fishing trawler that has been driven ashore at Land's End. The crew have been dramatically rescued by Breeches Buoy. This is a rescue procedure we have learnt in the Scouts.

As I enter the lower sixth form two events occur that result in me taking the notion that I might look to architecture as a career. Certainly the guidance has not been offered from the pompously named Public Schools Career Advisory Service. They have interviewed the whole of our dormitory and in our post mortem discussions we find all but three of us have been advised to go into forestry. An inspiring lecture from Truro architect John Crowther is closely followed by a casual moment one lunch time. Our large refectory tables accommodate five pupils each side on trestle benches with prefect as head of table. In the lower sixth I sit top right hand as deputy head of table and first for seconds of food. Our mail comes with lunch. One day I find my head of table sharing with me his career advice for architecture from the Royal Institute of British Architects. No, it's not for him. I have not received any post that day so I casually glance at his discarded information. There are thirty-eight schools of architecture in Britain and off I go to have a chat with Cyril Smith. His advice is that I apply to the Architectural Association in London. He understands it to be the oldest and probably the most respected of all the schools of architecture validated by the RIBA.

Uniform caps must be worn up to the fifth form, but are retained at the bottom of the trunk through the sixth form years for a special purpose. On the last Sunday of our careers at Truro we have the Caps Ceremony. This involves cutting off the peak, turning the cap inside out and using it to manufacture a mortar board fixing it with an oversize tassel. The last Sunday consists of final Morning service at St Mary's Methodist Church, followed by marching through the City to Boscawen Bridge where we stand in groups on the De Lank granite parapet. There is always a large assembled audience. To this audience we say or sing whatever we feel is a fitting epitaph to our school days. The mortar boards are flung into the Truro River and we watch them floating down towards Falmouth and the sea. They carry with them memories of boarding school and our dreams for the future.

My dreams are on their way up the river Thames, subject only to requisite A level results which are eagerly awaited. In the latter part of my boarding school days Mum and Dad have prepared for their retirement by buying Sheephouse Down, a handsome 1930s timber dwelling on the cliffs at Widemouth Bay, three miles south of Bude. It enjoys a magnificent south western aspect and glorious prospect looking down the coastline to Trevose Head in the far distance. Widemouth Bay is a charming, windswept coastal community. It has a post office and stores from where, one late summer morning, I receive a 6 am telephone

Marching through the City of Truro en route to Boscawen Bridge for our leavers ceremony. I am far left with tennis ball adorning my mortar board.

Photo Truro School / Ball family archive

call to say an envelope has arrived for me which looks as if it might be my A level results. Would I like to come and collect this, or wait until Postie's daily round? In this envelope is confirmation that the next chapter of my life will take me across the River Tamar.

As I pack my school trunk for the last time with its Truro School Inventory of junior days still sellotaped to the inside of the lid, what am I taking away from my seven years of boarding school life in Cornwall's Cathedral City? My recollection of this moment is the sudden dawning that time has a forward-only momentum. My boarding days are already history, a different and departing era of my life. One thing is certain. I have developed a passionate relationship with the land of Cornwall with all its ways and byways, its moods and mysteries. Being in close communion with Cornwall is to be a happy constant in my life. Just like my father before me I have already developed a reluctance to stray far from this land of my birth. The potent alchemy for me has been scouting, geology and archaeology, tramping around the Cornish Atlantic landscape with all its sepulchral Celtic fragments retaining their secrets

Never keep the human spirit from its road
Thro' landscape fresh upholstered and replete
This life is for the fearless, brave and bold
Not those who've ne'er known victory or defeat.

The end of my school days. Boscawen Bridge Truro July 1965. I am 2nd left with arm raised.
Photo Truro School / Ball family archive

Afterword

And so began my professional training at the Architectural Association in London. For seven years I was tutored in creative thinking and originality harnessing the arts and the sciences to imagineering the future. The imperative was to relate the technologies of the age to the issues of the age, to carry as our watchwords, the tenets of good design, firmness, commodity and delight and to ensure our proposals composed appropriately in their culture-specific landscapes and urban environments.

'Design with Beauty, Build in Truth', the motto of the Architectural Association, captures this essence. During my early AA training, Head of School William Allen became my guiding star just as Leonard Penna had been for me at Truro School. After graduation I returned to Bude in 1974 and established the Jonathan Ball Practice.

How serendipitous that in the year of my birth 1947, the necessities of time brought together the Ball and Cornish families. As I write Wroes of Bude is the largest family run department store in Cornwall, my brother Chris having assumed control when our parents retired and was subsequently joined in the business by my sister Jenny.

Since the 1970s when Teddy Hemmerle first took over H B H Woolacotts it has become the largest family run retail business in Cornwall. Each business now has retail outlets on both sides of the River Tamar. Both have second and third generation family members in control.

Looking back on my growing up years in Bude, I am struck by the happy constancy of life. More than 60 years later Bude remains one of the remotest of Cornwall's rural communities. Charm and resilience prosper hand in hand. Flooding still remains a seaborne hazard just as it was throughout my precious childhood years here in paradise.

Acknowledgements

This book started life in the most unusual circumstances. As the Millennium approached the difficulties concerning the evolution of the Eden Project had placed my life and that of my family in the most extreme peril.

I had the good fortune of having Mike Shaw, Literary Agent, then Chairman of Curtis Brown as chum and mentor. We had served together on the Committee of our London Club, the Athenaeum, Pall Mall. My first thanks must go to Mike for nurturing my writing ambition with his wise counsel which was to write, in the first instance, on my growing up years in Cornwall. This combined intimate knowledge with passion. My script was set aside by the ensuing Eden Project legal imbroglio and the subsequent writing of my own account as Eden Project co-founder, published as The Other Side of Eden, June 2014.

Revisiting my Cornish manuscript some months ago led me into many happy conversations with family and friends who have shared life here in the town we all love so well. Bude is one of those places which retains the enormous affection of its inhabitants. I am grateful to everyone who has contributed their memories. In particular I wish to thank my brother Chris and my sister Jenny, Teddy and Jean Hemmerle and Micky and Gertie Cornish together with Paddy Frost, all of whom most shared my early growing up years.

Special thanks go to Daniel Nanavati at FootSteps Press, my publisher and to Bob Willingham for cover design and all commissioned photographs. I must record a debt of gratitude to Adrian Abbott for making available his splendid photographic collection and to Steve Floyd from Truro School. Robert Godber and Terry Woodger have again been most generous with their time and have been invaluable in guiding me along the way.

To my PA Penelope Hasell I record heartfelt thanks in this happy task for more rigour being focused in validating recollection and in assisting my ambition that this story carries the hallmarks of cheerfulness and humour. Any mistakes are mine alone.

Finally, my wife Victoria who has put up with months of disruption at home with books and paperwork everywhere. Without her helpful observations my completed task would have been greatly diminished. Without her stalwart and unconditional support in my every endeavour I would be lost.

Bibliography

A Daughter's Tale by Mary Soames, pub. Doubleday, 2011

A Devon Family, the story of the Aclands, by Anne Acland, pub. Phillimore & Co, 1981

Bencoolen to Capricorno, a record of wrecks at Bude, by C.F.C. Bude Haven, pub J E Cornish, 1902

Bude Haven, Links with the Past, by Capt John E Acland, pub. Perry Bolt 1914

Cleave, by Bill Young, pub. privately 2001

Cornish Ballards and Other Poems by R S Hawker, Vicar of Morwenstow, pub. James Parker 1869, reprint 1904

Cornwall for Ever - Kernow bys Vyken - Edited by Philip Payton, pub. The Cornwall Millennium Committee, 2000

Footprints of Former Men of Cornwall by R S Hawker, pub. J Lane, 1903

Hawker of Morwenstow, by Piers Brendon, pub. Anthony Mott, 1975

High on the Hill, a history of Truro School by Joanna Wood, pub. Blue Hills Publishing, 2005

Laughter from Land's End by Arthur Caddick, printed privately 2004

Living Values, written and pub Brahma Kumaris, the World Spiritual University 1995

Odds and Ends, by the Rev. Wm Maskell, pub. James Toovey, 1872

Queen in Cornwall. a partial history of the world's greatest rock band, by Rupert White, pub. Antenna, 2011

Rugby in the Duchy by Kenneth Pelmear, pub. Cornwall RFU, 1960

Stories of Bude (3 volumes) John H Williams, pub privately 1992-1995

The Blanchminster Trust, a Cornish Charity by Kathleen Beswetherick, pub. The Blanchminster Trust 1991

The Book of Bude and Stratton, by Rennie Bere and Brian Dudley Stamp, pub. Barracuda Books, 1980

The Bude Branch by D J Wroe, pub. Kingfisher Railway Productions, 1988

The Church of St Morwenna and St John the Baptist, Morwenstow, by EWF Tomlin, pub. privately 1982

The Lynmouth Flood Disaster, by Eric Delderfield, pub. ERD Publications, 1953

The Malta Tramway and the Barracca Lift, by Joseph Bonnici and Michael Cassar, pub. by the authors, 1991

The Little Land of Cornwall, by A L Rowse, pub. Alan Sutton, 1986

The Principal Antiquities of the Land's End District, by Charles Thomas & Peter Pool, pub. The Cornwall Archaeological Society, 1962

The Story of Cornwall by A K Hamilton Jenkin, pub. Thomas Nelson & Sons, 1934

The Wreck at Sharp Nose Point by Jeremy Seal, pub. Picador, 2001

Under a Cornish Sky. The poetry of Arthur Caddick. Edited by Simon Parker. Pub. Scryfa 2008

Walls have Ears WFR Macartney, pub. Gollancz 1936

BBC Information and Archives, Your Life in their Hands. Part IV, Out on a Limb. Tx 04/03/58

Every effort has been made to credit all the owners of copyright, but if any omissions have occurred apologies are offered in advance and any mistakes in this respect will be rectified in any future editions of this book.

By the same author.
The Other Side of Eden. ISBN 978-1-908867-2-47

This is the story of one man's unflinching resolve and success in righting a public wrong, of a Cornishman looking to the glory of his nation and finding that enthusiasm, brilliant ideas and promises are not always enough.

"This story, of the extraordinary events which were part of the evolution of the Eden Project, reads like a legal thriller, and it will keep your attention to the end."
Sir David Brewer, Lord Lieutenant Greater London

www.jonathan-ball.com

Lightning Source UK Ltd.
Milton Keynes UK
UKOW07f0234080515

251090UK00002B/9/P